ITALIAN KITCHEN

Anna Del Conte
ITALIAN KITCHEN

PHOTOGRAPHS BY JASON LOWE

◙ SQUARE PEG

LONDON

SQUARE PEG

Published by Square Peg 2012
10 9 8 7 6 5 4 3 2 1

Copyright © Anna Del Conte

First published in Great Britain by Pavilion Books Ltd

Published in 2012 by Square Peg
Random House, 20 Vauxhall Bridge Road, London SW1V 2SA

www.rbooks.co.uk

Addresses for companies within The Random House Group Limited can be found at:
www.randomhouse.co.uk/offices.htm

The Random House Group Limited Reg. No. 954009

A CIP catalogue record for this book is available from the British Library

ISBN 9780224095365

The Random House Group Limited supports The Forest Stewardship Council® (FSC®), the
leading international forest certification organisation. Our books carrying the FSC label are
printed on FSC® certified paper. FSC is the only forest certification scheme endorsed by
the leading environmental organisations, including Greenpeace. Our paper procurement
policy can be found at www.randomhouse.co.uk/environment

Photography by Jason Lowe
Design by Anna Crone at www.siulendesign.com
Production by Anna Cowling

Printed and bound in China by C&C Offset Printing Co. Ltd

Contents

INTRODUCTION

This book is a compendium of four little books I wrote years ago which were published in 1993 by Pavilion. These were: *Antipasti*, *Pasta*, *Risotti* and *I Dolci*.

The first three books contained my favourite recipes of dishes for which Italian cooking is justly famous.

I decided to write the fourth one, *I Dolci*, for the opposite reason, i.e. because dolci – traditional Italian puddings, cakes, biscuits et al. – are not well known in Britain and some of them are well worth knowing.

Because of its nature, this book contains many vegetarian recipes.

ANTIPASTI

When I was taken out to dinner as a child I only ate *l'antipasto*. The trolley would be wheeled next to me and I would be transfixed by the beauty of the food and bewildered by the choice. After a few decades I still feel like that. I want to take all the dishes home, admire them, and eat them slowly and thoughtfully over the next few days. First a taste of prosciutto, as well as culatello and felino, my favourite salami, which I would eat with bread and nothing else. Next would come a few floppy slices of grilled peppers, a curly tentacle of *calameretti*, and a morsel of each stuffed vegetable. Finally, a spoonful of *nervetti in insalata* – Milanese brawn – gleaming with olive oil and crowned with colourful *sottaceti* – vegetables preserved in vinegar – and speckled with purple olives and minuscule green capers.

Such are the delights of an antipasto offered in a restaurant. When you serve antipasti at home, however, you must be more selective and decide on two or three dishes at most. Otherwise you will be in the kitchen for far too long and begin to hate the idea of an antipasto for ever.

An antipasto can provide a good beginning to a meal, and it can even set the style for the meal itself. It is very important that, as an opening to the meal, it should be well presented and pretty to look at. It should also be light and fresh, so as to develop the taste buds for the courses to follow, rather than fill the stomach, and it should harmonise with the rest of the meal.

Nowadays an antipasto is usually a starter, no longer followed by a *primo* – first course – except on special occasions. For instance, if you have decided on a platter of *affettato misto* – mixed cured meats – a generous bowl of tagliatelle dressed with a vigorous sauce would make an ideal follow-on. So also would an earthy risotto or a gutsy spaghetti *alla puttanesca* – with tomatoes, anchovies and chilli. This is not the traditional Italian way, but it is what suits our smaller stomachs and the preachings of the health gurus.

If, however, you are serving a joint of meat, start with a vegetable-based antipasto or a fish one. A fish antipasto, indeed, is the ideal precursor to a fish main course.

The recipes collected here are divided into six sections: Salumi, Bruschetta and Crostini, Salads, Stuffed Vegetables, Fish and Meat Antipasti, and Other Favourites.

Some of the recipes are for classic antipasto dishes, others are my own or those of my family and friends. All are typically Italian yet very varied. As varied, indeed, as most Italian cooking, because of the great differences between its many regions.

Salumi
CURED MEAT PRODUCTS

I know I am an unashamed chauvinist where food is concerned, but I am sure no other country offers such an array of delectable cured meats as Italy does. Salumi are usually made with pork or a mixture of pork and beef. There are also good salumi made with venison and various other meats. The mocetta from Valle d'Aosta is made with wild goat, the bresaola from Valtellina with fillet of beef, the salame d'oca from Friuli and Veneto with goose, and the salami and prosciutti di cinghiale are made with wild boar. This latter is one of the many glories of Tuscany.

The characteristics of the many types of salumi are determined firstly by factors affecting the pig, or other animal, itself. These include its breed, its habitat and food, and the climate of the locality in which it is reared. A prosciutto di Parma is paler and sweeter than, for instance, a prosciutto di montagna – mountain prosciutto. Secondly, salumi differ according to which cuts of meat are used, the proportion of fat to lean, the fineness of the mincing, the flavourings and the curing. In what follows I describe some of the salumi that I like to serve as an antipasto. Together they form a dish called *affettato misto*, possibly the most common antipasto served in Italy. This dish of mixed cured meats is pretty to look at in its shades of pink and red, and one of the most appetising ways to start a meal. You may be serving the *affettato* before a dish of pasta. (This is where I should point out that the word antipasto does not mean before the pasta. It means before the '*pasto*' – meal.) In Italy, however, *affettato* is often served as a *secondo* for lunch, not before but after the pasta that is de rigueur (only for lunch, though) in any self-respecting Italian family. Still, *primo* or *secondo*, *affettato misto* is an excellent dish, which, with some good bread or a piece of focaccia, followed by a lovely green salad and some cheese, is a perfect meal in its own right.

A good *affettato misto* should have a choice of at least five or six different meats. The following is a list of the products you can most easily find in Britain. You can mix them to your liking, but one type of prosciutto and two types of salami should always be included. With a prosciutto I put two or three different kinds of salami: one from northern Italy, a Milano perhaps, which is mild and sweet, a peppery salame from the south and a Roman oval-shaped soppressata. An alternative that I like is a fennel-flavoured finocchiona, a salame from Tuscany. A few slices of the best mortadella, speckled with the acid green of fresh pistachio nuts, and of tasty coppa, which is a rolled, cured and boned shoulder of pork, would be just right for a good assortment.

The prosciutto can be prosciutto di Parma, the sweetest and palest of them all, or prosciutto di San Daniele, made in Friuli, of a darker red and stronger flavour. There is also a prosciutto di Carpegna, which is available in some of the best Italian delicatessens. I like it because it has a good flavour, is usually perfectly salted and contains the right amount of fat. A good prosciutto should always have some fat.

As for the quantity, I find that about 60g per person is enough. However, it is probably a good idea to buy more, because if you have a few slices left over they come in very handy for a sandwich the next day.

Try to buy your salumi from a delicatessen where it is sliced in front of you, rather than in vacuum packs from a supermarket. It is usually a better product and you can see with your own eyes if it is really the salumi it purports to be. For instance, prosciutti have a mark of origin, their DOC, stamped on the skin. If you ask for the salumi to be sliced, remember that prosciutto should be sliced fine, but not so fine that you cannot transfer the slice to a dish without breaking it. Salami are better thicker, and the smaller the diameter of the salame, the thicker the cut should be.

Bruschetta e Crostini
GRILLED AND TOASTED BREAD

Bruschetta and crostini are very popular antipasti, not just in Italy but in Britain too, and make good 'finger food'. It is fundamental to the quality of either to use a good chewy type of bread – ciabatta, sourdough or pain rustique for example. Here are some classic Italian recipes.

In Italy, crostini cover a broader range of dishes than bruschetta. Crostini consist of slices of toasted bread moistened with olive oil on which different toppings are spread, while bruschetta is either grilled country bread flavoured with olive oil and garlic, or the same grilled bread topped with tomato.

Bruschetta
ROMAN GARLIC BREAD

Bruschetta is a crisp, charred-tasting bread, originally from Rome (*bruscare* means 'to burn lightly' in Roman dialect). It is made with coarse country bread, which has a high nutritional value. For centuries bruschetta has been a staple dish of the poor, who ironically used to call it *cappone* – capon – since it was the nearest they could get to this delicacy of the rich. Nowadays bruschetta is served as an appetiser while you wait for your pasta to be ready. Bruschetta is also ideal to eat with fish soups.

To make bruschetta cut a good loaf of white bread – ciabatta, Pugliese, pain de campagne or sourdough – into thick (1.5–2cm) slices. For 6 slices you will need 2–3 squashed garlic cloves, some extra virgin olive oil, preferably a peppery Tuscan oil, and a good deal of freshly ground black pepper.

Score the slices lightly with the point of a small knife in a criss-cross fashion. Grill the bread on both sides over charcoal or wood embers (or under the grill) and then, while still hot, rub it with the garlic. Put the slices in a hot oven for 2 minutes, to make them crisp through, and then place them on a dish. Drizzle about 1 tbsp of oil over each one and sprinkle generously with pepper and a little sea salt.

Bruschetta Tradizionale
CLASSIC BRUSCHETTA

Serves 4

6 tomatoes
sea salt
1 ciabatta loaf
2–3 garlic cloves, cut into
  large pieces
2–3 tbsp extra virgin olive oil
freshly ground black pepper
12 basil leaves, torn into
  large pieces

1 Wash and dry the tomatoes. Cut them into small pieces, put on a wooden board and sprinkle with a little salt, which will bring out the flavour. Leave them for about 30–40 minutes.

2 Prepare the bruschetta following the instructions on page 19 and dress it with the garlic and the oil. Pick up the pieces of tomatoes, leaving the juice behind, and put them on the grilled and dressed bread.

3 Drizzle a ½ tsp of olive oil over each bruschetta and place a few pieces of basil on top.

Bruschetta is now part of the British culinary repertoire. My only reservation is that bruschetta with tomatoes can only be made with good tomatoes – ripe, sweet, yet full of flavour and with a thin skin, since the tomatoes must not be peeled. Plum tomatoes are particularly suitable, because they do not have many seeds. For the bread, I usually use ciabatta, which is the right-sized loaf.

Crostini alla Toscana
CHICKEN LIVER CROSTINI

Serves 6–8

225g chicken livers
4 tbsp olive oil (for cooking)
½ celery stick, very finely
  chopped
1 shallot, very finely chopped
2 small garlic cloves, chopped
3 tbsp chopped flat-leaf parsley
100g lean minced beef
1 tbsp tomato purée
6 tbsp dry white wine
sea salt and freshly ground
  black pepper
1 tbsp capers, rinsed and
  chopped
2 salted anchovies, boned and
  rinsed, or 4 canned anchovy
  fillets, chopped
30g unsalted butter

1 Remove the fat, gristle and any greenish bits from the chicken livers. Wash, dry and chop as finely as you can.

2 Put the olive oil in a saucepan and, when just hot, add the celery, shallot, garlic and parsley. Cook for 10 minutes until soft, stirring very frequently.

3 Add the chicken livers and the mince and cook very gently until the chicken livers have lost their raw colour and have become crumbly.

4 Mix in the tomato purée and cook for 1 minute. Raise the heat, pour over the wine and boil to reduce until nearly all the wine has evaporated. Lower the heat and add a little salt and plenty of pepper. Simmer gently for 30 minutes, adding a little hot water if the mixture gets too dry.

5 Mix in the capers and the anchovies. Add the butter and cook gently for 5 minutes, stirring constantly.

6 Spread the mixture on crostini (see page 18) moistened with olive oil or with a mixture of good chicken stock and vinsanto.

In Tuscany, where this dish comes from, they add calf's melt (the spleen) to the chicken liver. Melt is added only to tone down the flavour of the liver and to give the mixture more volume. Of all offal, melt is the only one that is always used with other types of offal. To give this extra consistency to the mixture I have substituted minced beef for the melt. It works very well.

You can moisten the bread with vinsanto mixed with stock, instead of the more common olive oil. Vinsanto is a very strong wine from Chianti, made from grapes that are left to dry for several weeks before they are pressed.

Pure di Fave
BROAD BEAN PURÉE

Serves 6–8

1.35kg fresh broad beans,
  or 450g frozen broad beans
sea salt and freshly ground
  black pepper
3 garlic cloves, peeled
60g good-quality crustless
  white bread
milk
90ml extra virgin olive oil

1   Shell the broad beans, if you are using fresh ones. Cook the fresh or frozen beans in a saucepan of simmering water to which you have added 1 tbsp of salt and the garlic. The beans should cook at the lowest simmer. When the beans are tender, drain them and the garlic, reserving a cupful of the water. Allow to cool.

2   Put the bread in a bowl and pour in enough milk just to cover the bread.

3   Now you should have the patience to slip off the white skin from the beans. It's rather a boring and lengthy job, but it is necessary if you want a really creamy purée without those unpleasant pieces of papery skin. If there are any children around the house enlist their help; they usually love popping the beans out of their skin.

4   Put the broad beans, garlic and bread with its milk in a food processor and whizz to a purée, while gradually adding all but about 1 tbsp of the oil through the funnel. Taste and adjust the seasoning, adding a little of the reserved water if too thick.

5   You can spread the purée on crostini (see page 18) moistened with the reserved oil, or serve the purée piled up in a dish surrounded by crostini, and let your guests or family do the work.

For this recipe you can use frozen broad beans which, although they do not have all the sweet mealiness of fresh ones, are picked and frozen at their best. Some recipes suggest using boiled potatoes instead of the bread. Either version is good.

Intingolo di Peperoni e Pomodori Secchi

RELISH OF PEPPERS AND SUN-DRIED TOMATOES

Serves 4

2 tbsp red wine vinegar
2 large red and/or yellow
 peppers
½ sweet onion, very finely
 chopped
2 tbsp extra virgin olive oil
1 garlic clove, very finely
 chopped
½ dried chilli, crumbled
2 tsp balsamic vinegar
200g sun-dried tomatoes
 in olive oil
1 canned anchovy fillet,
 chopped
1 tbsp capers, rinsed and dried
sea salt and freshly ground
 black pepper

1   Heat the oven to 230°C/Gas Mark 8.

2   Put the peppers on a baking tray and roast in the oven until they are soft, about 30 minutes. Remove from the oven and allow to cool a little.

3   Meanwhile, heat the onion and oil in a small frying pan. Sauté for a few minutes and then add the garlic, chilli and balsamic vinegar, so that the *soffritto* (frying mixture) does not catch. Continue cooking until very soft, stirring frequently.

4   Drain the tomatoes of their preserving oil, cut them into thin strips and chuck them into the *soffritto*. Cook, stirring frequently, for 5 minutes or so.

5   While the tomatoes are cooking, peel the peppers, cut them in half and discard the core and seeds. Cut them into 1cm pieces and mix into the *soffritto* in the pan. Let the peppers *insaporire* – take up the flavour.

6   Add the anchovy fillet to the pan and squash it down to a purée. Mix in the capers. Taste and adjust the seasoning. Serve warm or cold.

Fonduta Piemontese
PIEDMONTESE FONDUE

Serves 4

400g Italian fontina
250ml full-fat milk
60g unsalted butter
4 large egg yolks
1 white truffle, or
1 tbsp truffle paste

1 About 6 hours before you want to serve the fonduta, cut the fontina into small dice. Put in a bowl and add enough milk just to cover the cheese. Set aside.

2 Put the butter in a heatproof bowl, add the fontina with the milk and set over a pan of simmering water.

3 Cook, stirring constantly, for about 10 minutes until the cheese has melted, then beat in the egg yolks, one at a time. Continue cooking, beating the whole time, until the egg has been absorbed and the sauce reaches the consistency of double cream. If you are using truffle paste, mix it in at this point, off the heat.

4 Transfer the fonduta to individual soup dishes and slice the truffle over it, if you are using this food of the gods. Serve immediately.

Fontina, the best-known cheese from Valle d'Aosta, used to be made at Mont Fontin, from which it takes its name. It is the main ingredient of this classic dish. The other characteristic ingredient is the white truffle of Alba. There are now various brands of truffle paste on the market, made with white truffles and porcini, which works very well in a fonduta. Sliced bread or crostini (see page 18) are served with fonduta for dipping into it. I also like to use thick slices of grilled polenta.

Insalate
SALADS

A mixed antipasto for a large party, or an antipasto
table in a restaurant, usually contains a number
of different salads. Grilled peppers, for instance,
are a classic antipasto salad, as are tomatoes with
mozzarella and basil. The following five recipes
include some of my favourites and some classics.

Insalata di Pere e Formaggio
PEAR AND CHEESE SALAD

Serves 4

4 ripe Williams or Comice
 pears
100g Parmigiano-Reggiano
 or good padano cheese
100g mature pecorino
3 tbsp extra virgin olive oil
2 tbsp lemon juice
sea salt and freshly ground
 black pepper
120g rocket

1 Peel the pears, cut them into quarters and remove the cores. Cut each quarter in half and put them in a bowl.
2 Shave the cheese with a vegetable peeler and mix three-quarters of it with the pears.
3 Beat the oil and the lemon juice together and add salt and pepper to taste. Spoon about half this dressing over the pears and leave for 1 hour.
4 Spoon the pears into a deep dish and shower with the remaining cheese. Surround with the rocket and drizzle the rest of the dressing over it. Serve immediately.

We have a saying in Italy, 'Do not let the peasant know how good pears are with cheese' – or he might pick all the pears off your tree. This salad is a sophisticated version of the classic pears with cheese.

Insalata di Broccoli con la Mollica
BROCCOLI AND BREADCRUMB SALAD

Serves 4

450g broccoli
6 tbsp extra virgin olive oil
125g fresh breadcrumbs
6 canned anchovy fillets,
  drained, or 3 salted
  anchovies, boned and rinsed
1 or 2 dried chillies, according
  to taste, seeded
2 garlic cloves, peeled
1½ tbsp capers, rinsed and
  dried
12 black olives, stoned and
  cut into strips
sea salt and freshly ground
  black pepper

1 Divide the broccoli into small florets. Peel the outer layer from the stalks and cut them into small pieces. Blanch the florets and pieces of stalk in boiling salted water until just tender, about 5 minutes. Drain and dry with kitchen paper. Transfer to a bowl and add 2 tbsp of the oil. Toss gently using 2 forks, rather than spoons, as they are less likely to break the florets.

2 Heat the rest of the oil in a frying pan and add the breadcrumbs. Cook for 3 minutes, stirring to coat them with the oil.

3 Chop all the other ingredients, except the olives, and add them to the bread mixture. Add the olives and cook for another minute or so, stirring well. Taste and add salt and pepper as necessary.

4 Toss half the breadcrumb mixture into the broccoli and spoon the rest over the top. Serve warm.

Brown breadcrumbs are better than white for this tasty dish from southern Italy. I make my soft crumbs in a food processor, a very quick job. You can use cauliflower instead of broccoli.

Peperoni Arrostiti
GRILLED PEPPERS

Serves 4

4 beautiful red or yellow
  peppers
6 canned anchovy fillets,
  drained, or 3 salted
  anchovies, boned and rinsed
3 garlic cloves
2 tbsp chopped flat-leaf parsley
1 small dried chilli, seeded
4 tbsp extra virgin olive oil

1   Hold the peppers over the flame of a burner or put them under
the grill and grill them all over. When the side in contact with the heat
is charred, turn the pepper, until all the surface, including the top and
bottom, is charred. As soon as all the skin is charred, take the pepper
from the heat, otherwise the flesh will begin to burn and you will be left
with paper-thin peppers.

2   Let the peppers cool and then remove the skin; it will come off very
easily as long as the peppers have been well charred. Cut the peppers in
half, remove the stalk and seeds and then cut them lengthways into strips.
Put them on a dish.

3   Pound the anchovies with the garlic, parsley and chilli in a mortar,
or chop very finely.

4   Put the oil and the anchovy mixture in a very heavy pan and heat very
slowly for about 2 minutes, stirring and pounding the whole time until the
mixture is mashed. Spoon over the peppers and leave to marinate for at
least 4 hours. The longer you leave them – up to a week – the better they
get. Serve plenty of bread with them.

When peppers are grilled and skinned their taste is
totally different from that of raw or sautéed peppers.
To my mind they are much nicer, and they are certainly
more digestible. You can prepare a few kilos of peppers
when they are in season, and reasonably cheap, and
keep them in the fridge in jars, well covered with olive
oil, for 2 or 3 months.

Pomodori con la Mozzarella e il Basilico
TOMATOES, MOZZARELLA AND BASIL

Serves 4

12 ripe tomatoes
sea salt and freshly ground
 black pepper
350g buffalo mozzarella
6 tbsp extra virgin olive oil
24 fresh basil leaves

1   Wash and dry the tomatoes and cut them in half. Squeeze out a little of the seeds and juice and sprinkle with salt. Lay the tomato halves on a wooden board, cut side down. Put the board in the fridge and leave for at least 30 minutes.

2   Wipe the inside of the tomatoes with kitchen paper and place them, cut side up, on a dish.

3   Cut the mozzarella into 24 slices or pieces. Put 1 piece inside each tomato half. Season with a generous grinding of pepper and drizzle with the olive oil.

4   Wipe the basil leaves with a moistened piece of kitchen paper. Place a leaf over each piece of mozzarella.

This is the simplest and best summer antipasto. However, do not do it unless you have very good tomatoes – tasty and juicy, not woolly and dry. Sometimes you can buy the best round tomatoes from Calabria or Campania, sold still attached to their branches. Also, use buffalo mozzarella, which has a much deeper flavour than cow's milk mozzarella.

Panzanella
BREAD AND RAW VEGETABLE SALAD

Serves 4

8 thick slices of chewy
 country-style white bread
2–3 tbsp white wine vinegar
12 fresh basil leaves,
 coarsely torn
2 garlic cloves, peeled and
 finely chopped
½ cucumber, peeled and cut
 into 1cm slices
½ red onion, very thinly sliced
225g ripe meaty tomatoes,
 seeded and cut into 1cm cubes
sea salt and freshly ground
 black pepper
6 tbsp extra virgin olive oil

1 Cover the bread with cold water to which you have added 1 tbsp of the vinegar. Leave to soak until just soft, then squeeze out all the liquid and put the bread in a salad bowl. The bread should be damp but not wet. Break it up with a fork.

2 Add the basil, garlic, cucumber, onion and tomatoes. Season with salt and pepper. Toss thoroughly with the oil, using a fork to turn the mixture over. Chill for 30 minutes or so.

3 Taste and add more vinegar to your liking. It is not possible to specify the amount of vinegar to use, since it depends on its acidity and on personal taste.

A traditional rustic salad made in the summer with country bread and seasonal raw vegetables. Make it only when good tomatoes are in season, and with country-type bread. I recommend a Pugliese loaf, available in good supermarkets or in Italian delicatessens.

Verdure Ripiene
STUFFED VEGETABLES

One of the joys of walking around the old part of
Genoa is that you can still see shops selling farinata
(chickpea tart), focaccia, pissaladeira (onion pizza) and
stuffed vegetables, all in the huge round copper pans
in which they have been baked. Fat red tomatoes and
shimmering red and yellow peppers fight for space with
aubergines, of all colours from purple to ivory, and
plump round courgettes, all soft and glistening with oil.
The recipes that follow are for my favourite stuffed
vegetables. If you choose two or three of them and
serve them together you are sure to give your family
and friends one of the most appetising and satisfying
antipasti ever.

The tomatoes, peppers and courgettes, for instance,
go together very well, while the aubergines are perfect
also by themselves. All these stuffed vegetables are best
served warm or at room temperature, but not hot or
chilled. They are even more delicious if made a day
in advance.

Funghetti Ripieni alla Genovese
STUFFED MUSHROOM CAPS

Serves 4

20g dried porcini
450g large-cap mushrooms
45g fresh white breadcrumbs
1 salted anchovy, boned and
  rinsed, or 2 canned anchovy
  fillets
1 or 2 garlic cloves, according
  to taste, peeled
handful of fresh marjoram
pinch of grated nutmeg
sea salt and freshly ground
  black pepper
4 tbsp extra virgin olive oil
2 tbsp chopped flat-leaf parsley

1 Soak the dried porcini in a cupful of very hot water for 30 minutes. If necessary, rinse under cold water to remove any trace of grit. Dry thoroughly with kitchen paper.
2 Gently wipe the large-cap mushrooms with a damp cloth and detach the stalks.
3 Chop together the dried porcini, mushroom stalks, breadcrumbs, anchovies, garlic and marjoram. You can use a food processor, but do not reduce to pulp. Transfer to a bowl and add the nutmeg and salt and pepper to taste.
4 Heat the oven to 220°C/Gas Mark 7.
5 Heat 2 tbsp of the oil in a frying pan and add the mushroom and breadcrumb mixture. Sauté for 5 minutes, stirring frequently.
6 Lay the mushroom caps on an oiled baking tray, hollow side up. Sprinkle them with salt and then fill them with the crumb mixture. Sprinkle a pinch or two of parsley on top of each cap and then drizzle with the remaining oil. Bake for 10–15 minutes until the caps are soft. Serve at room temperature.

If you can find them, use fresh porcini (ceps). Otherwise you can use cultivated large mushrooms, plus a little dried porcini for better flavour, as in this recipe.

Melanzane Ripiene
AUBERGINE STUFFED WITH SAUSAGE, PINE NUTS AND CURRANTS

Serves 4

2 aubergines, about 450g each
sea salt and freshly ground
  black pepper
4 tbsp extra virgin olive oil
1 large garlic clove, finely
  chopped
½ small onion or 1 shallot,
  very finely chopped
½ celery stick, very finely
  chopped
225g spicy luganega or other
  spicy coarse-grained pure
  pork continental sausage,
  skinned and crumbled
30g soft white breadcrumbs
3 tbsp pine nuts
2 tbsp capers, rinsed and dried
1 large egg
1 tbsp dried oregano
3 tbsp freshly grated pecorino
  or Parmesan
3 tbsp dried currants
1 large ripe tomato

1 Wash and dry the aubergines. Cut them in half lengthways and scoop out all the flesh with the help of a small sharp knife and then with a small teaspoon, leaving just enough pulp to cover the skin. Be careful not to pierce the skin.

2 Chop the pulp of the aubergine coarsely and place in a colander. Sprinkle with salt, mix well and leave to drain for about 1 hour.

3 Heat the oven to 190°C/Gas Mark 5.

4 Put 3 tbsp of the oil, the garlic, onion and celery in a frying pan and sauté over a low heat until soft, stirring frequently. Add the sausage and cook for 20 minutes, turning it over frequently.

5 Meanwhile, squeeze the liquid from the chopped aubergine pulp and dry thoroughly with kitchen paper. Add the aubergine pulp to the pan and fry gently for a few minutes, stirring frequently. Taste and adjust the seasoning.

6 Add the breadcrumbs to the mixture in the frying pan. After 2–3 minutes, mix in the pine nuts. Cook for a further 30 seconds, then transfer to a bowl.

7 Add the capers, egg, oregano, cheese, currants and pepper to taste to the mixture in the bowl and mix very thoroughly. Taste and add salt if necessary.

8 Pat dry the inside of the aubergine shells. Oil a baking dish large enough to hold the aubergine shells in a single layer. Place the aubergine shells, one next to the other, in the dish and fill them with the sausage mixture.

9 Cut the tomato into strips and place 2 or 3 strips on the top of each aubergine half. Drizzle with the rest of the oil. Add 120ml of water to the bottom of the dish. Cover the dish tightly with foil and bake for 20 minutes. Remove the foil and bake for a further 20 minutes. This dish is best eaten warm, an hour or so after it comes out of the oven.

Pomodori Ammollicati

TOMATOES STUFFED WITH BREADCRUMBS AND PARSLEY

Serves 3 or 4

6 large round tomatoes,
 ripe but firm
sea salt and freshly ground
 black pepper
2 tbsp chopped flat-leaf parsley
2 garlic cloves, finely chopped
1 tbsp capers, rinsed and
 chopped
½ small dried chilli, chopped
4 tbsp dried white breadcrumbs
½ tbsp dried oregano
5 tbsp extra virgin olive oil

1 Cut the tomatoes in half. Remove the seeds and sprinkle with salt. Lay them cut side down on a wooden board to drain for about 30 minutes. Wipe the inside of each half with kitchen paper.

2 Heat the oven to 180°C/Gas Mark 4.

3 Put the parsley, garlic, capers, chilli, breadcrumbs and oregano in a bowl. Mix well and then add 4 tbsp of the oil. Season with a little salt and some pepper. Mix well to a paste.

4 Oil the bottom of a shallow baking dish or roasting tin. Place the tomatoes in the dish, cut side up.

5 Spoon a little of the breadcrumb mixture into each half tomato and drizzle the rest of the oil over the top. Bake for about 30 minutes until the tomatoes are soft but still whole. Serve at room temperature.

Peperoni Ammollicati
PEPPERS STUFFED WITH BREADCRUMBS AND PARSLEY

Serves 4

700g red and yellow peppers
5 tbsp extra virgin olive oil
sea salt and freshly ground
 black pepper
3 tbsp chopped flat-leaf parsley
2 garlic cloves, finely chopped
1 tbsp capers, rinsed and
 chopped
½ small dried chilli, chopped
2 salted anchovies, boned,
 rinsed and chopped
4 tbsp dried white breadcrumbs

1 Heat the oven to 180°C/Gas Mark 4.
2 Cut the peppers into quarters and remove the cores, ribs and seeds. Heat 4 tbsp of the oil in a large frying pan until very hot and then add the peppers, skin side down. Sprinkle with salt and pepper and cook for about 10 minutes, shaking the pan occasionally.
3 Mix together the remaining ingredients in a bowl.
4 When the peppers are just soft, place them in an oiled baking dish, cut side up. Pour the juices from the pan into the breadcrumb mixture and mix well. Taste and check the seasoning.
5 Place a small mound of stuffing into each piece of pepper, drizzle with the remaining oil and bake for 15 minutes.

The stuffing for peppers is basically the same as that for tomatoes. I prefer, however, to omit the oregano and to add salted anchovies. Use red and yellow peppers, but not green because they are not sweet enough.

Zucchine al Forno
BAKED COURGETTES WITH MINT AND GARLIC STUFFING

Serves 4

450g medium courgettes
sea salt and freshly ground
 black pepper
2 tbsp chopped flat-leaf parsley
4 tbsp chopped fresh mint
2 garlic cloves, chopped
4 tbsp dried breadcrumbs
6 tbsp extra virgin olive oil

1   Cut the courgettes in half lengthways. Make some diagonal incisions on the cut side. Sprinkle the cut side lightly with salt and place the courgette halves on a wooden board, cut side down. This will allow some of the liquid to drain away.

2   Heat the oven to 180°C/Gas Mark 4.

3   Put the chopped herbs in a bowl and add the garlic and breadcrumbs. Add half the oil gradually, while beating with a fork. Season with a good grinding of pepper and with very little salt.

4   Oil a shallow baking dish or a lasagne dish large enough to hold all the courgette halves in a single layer.

5   Wipe the courgettes with kitchen paper and lay them in the dish, cut side up. Spoon a little of the herb mixture over each half. Drizzle 1 tbsp of the oil over the halves and cover the dish with foil. Bake for 15 minutes. Remove the foil and continue baking until the courgettes are tender and the top is crisp, about 10 minutes longer.

6   Drizzle with the remaining oil while the courgettes are still hot. Serve warm or at room temperature.

Antipasti di Pesce e Carne
FISH AND MEAT ANTIPASTI

The following recipes are for dishes whose main
ingredient, whether fish or meat, is usually served
as a main course. In these recipes the fish and meat
is prepared in a light and lively way that is extremely
appetising and therefore particularly suited to an
antipasto.

Cozze Ripiene
STUFFED MUSSELS

Serves 4

900g mussels
2 organic lemons, cut into
 quarters
6 garlic cloves, peeled
120ml extra virgin olive oil
5 tbsp chopped flat-leaf parsley
5 tbsp dried breadcrumbs
sea salt and freshly ground
 black pepper

1 Mussels are much cleaner these days, because they are usually farmed. However, they still need a good cleaning. Put them in a sink full of cold water and scrub them with a stiff brush. Scrape off any barnacles and beards. Discard any mussel that stays open after tapping it against a hard surface: it is dead. Rinse the mussels in several changes of water until the water is clean, and no sand is left at the bottom of the sink.

2 Put the lemon quarters and 5 cloves of garlic in a large frying pan. Add the mussels, cover and cook over a high heat until the mussels are open. Shake the pan occasionally. (Discard any that remain closed. They might be full of sand.)

3 Heat the oven to 220°C/Gas Mark 7.

4 Remove the top of each mussel shell. Loosen the mussels in the bottom shell and place them on a baking tray.

5 Filter the mussel liquid left in the pan through a sieve lined with muslin into a bowl. Mix in the oil, parsley, breadcrumbs, and salt and pepper to taste. Finely chop the remaining garlic and add to the mixture.

6 Place a little of the parsley and breadcrumb mixture over each mussel and bake for about 7 minutes until golden brown.

This is the basic recipe for cozze ripiene, to which other ingredients such as grated pecorino, tomato sauce, capers and so on can be added.

Insalata Calda di Mare
WARM SEAFOOD SALAD

In this popular antipasto dish you can vary the fish you use according to your taste and the availability of the fish in the market. Remember to have a good selection of textures, but do not use any kind of blue fish as its taste would be too strong.
I like to serve this seafood salad warm.

Serves 6

450g mussels
1 dried chilli, left whole
450g squid
4 tbsp wine vinegar
1 onion, cut in half
2 bay leaves
sea salt and freshly ground
 black pepper
350g monkfish
225g shelled scallops
12 large raw prawns in shell,
 about 225g
1 garlic clove, finely chopped
3 tbsp chopped flat-leaf parsley
3 tbsp lemon juice
150ml extra virgin olive oil
black olives, to garnish

1   Put the mussels in a sink full of cold water and scrub them with a stiff brush, scraping off any barnacles and beards with a small knife. Discard any open mussel that fails to close after being tapped hard on a hard surface. Rinse the mussels in several changes of water until the water is clean and no sand is left at the bottom of the sink.

2   Put the mussels in a large saucepan, cover and cook over a high heat until they are open, shaking the pan every now and then. (Discard any mussels that remain closed.) Shell the mussels and put the meat in a bowl; discard the shells. If there is sand in the liquid, filter the liquid through a fine sieve, then pour the clear liquid over the mussels. Pour it very gently so that any sand is left on the bottom of the pan. Add the chilli for flavouring.

3   Ask your fishmonger to clean and skin the squid. If he is not prepared to do it, proceed as follows. Hold the sac in one hand and pull off the tentacles with the other hand. The contents of the sac will come out too. Cut the tentacles above the eyes. Squeeze out the thin bony beak in the centre of the tentacles. Peel off the skin from the sac and the flap. Remove the translucent backbone from inside the sac and rinse the sac and tentacles under cold water. Cut the sac into strips and the tentacles into bite-sized pieces.

4 Put about 1.5 litres of cold water in a saucepan, add 2 tbsp of the vinegar, the onion, 1 bay leaf and some salt and bring to the boil. Add the squid and cook over a steady simmer for 5–15 minutes, depending on their size. Squid are cooked when they become white and lose their translucency and you can pierce them with a fork. Remove the squid from the water with a slotted spoon, drain well and add to the mussels in the bowl.

5 Cut the monkfish into large chunks and add to the boiling water in which the squid have cooked. Simmer gently for about 2 minutes. Remove from the heat, leaving the fish in the liquid.

6 While the monkfish is cooking, put another saucepan on the heat with about 600ml of hot water, the remaining bay leaf, the rest of the vinegar and some salt. When the water is boiling, add the scallops. Simmer for 2 minutes after the water has returned to the boil and then remove with a slotted spoon. If the scallops are large, cut them into quarters. Add to the bowl containing the mussels and squid.

7 Put the prawns into the boiling water in which the scallops have cooked. Simmer for 1 minute after the water has come back to the boil. Drain and set aside to cool.

8 Drain the monkfish. Remove any bone and skin and cut into bite-sized pieces. Add the fish to the bowl with the other seafood.

9 Peel the prawns and, if necessary, devein them. Cut them into rounds and add to the bowl.

10 Prepare the sauce: mix the garlic, parsley and lemon juice together in a small bowl. Add a generous grinding of black pepper and some salt. Beat in the oil slowly. Taste and adjust the seasonings.

11 Before serving, put the bowl containing the seafood over a saucepan of simmering water. Cover the bowl and heat until the fish is warm, not hot. Stir it once or twice, using a fork, not a spoon, which would tend to break the pieces of fish.

12 Fish the chilli out of the bowl and discard it. Spoon the sauce over the seafood and toss gently but thoroughly. Pile the seafood salad in a deep dish and scatter the olives over it.

Magroni di Anatra all'Aceto Balsamico
DUCK BREASTS WITH BALSAMIC VINEGAR

Serves 6

2 duck breasts, about
 350g each
sea salt and freshly ground
 black pepper
2–3 tbsp balsamic vinegar,
 according to taste and acidity
225g lamb's lettuce
3 tbsp extra virgin olive oil

1 Score the skin of the duck breasts with the point of a small sharp knife. Rub with salt and pepper.

2 Heat a frying pan. Place the breasts in the pan, skin side down, and cook over a moderate heat for 7–9 minutes, depending on their thickness. The fat will run out. Pour out nearly all the fat (keep it for sauté potatoes).

3 Spoon 1 tbsp of balsamic vinegar over the breasts and turn them over. Cook for 2 minutes on the underside. Lift out the breasts and place on a board. Carve across into 5mm slices. Place the slices on a warm dish. Cover with foil and leave for 10 minutes, for the muscle to relax.

4 Add the remaining balsamic vinegar and about 4 tbsp of hot water to the frying pan and stir well to deglaze the juices. Taste to see if you need a little more vinegar and/or a little more water.

5 Toss the lamb's lettuce with the oil and season with a little salt and a generous grinding of pepper. Make a bed of lamb's lettuce on each plate.

6 Place the duck slices on the lamb's lettuce and pour over the juices from the pan. Do not wait too long to serve the dish after you have poured the juices or the lettuce will 'tire' too much.

Balsamic vinegar is a superb condiment for duck. The sauce it produces when mixed with the cooking juices is rich in flavour and yet tangy enough to cut across the richness of the meat. I like to serve this duck with a light salad of lamb's lettuce as its lemony flavour and fresh crispness tone down the fattiness of the duck. If you cannot find lamb's lettuce, use curly endive, cut into thin strips.

Sarde a Beccaficu
STUFFED SARDINES

Serves 6

900g fresh sardines
4 level tbsp dried currants
5 tbsp olive oil
75g dried white breadcrumbs
4 level tbsp pine nuts
1 garlic clove, finely chopped
2 level tbsp chopped flat-leaf
  parsley
2 level tbsp grated mature
  pecorino
sea salt and freshly ground
  black pepper
12 bay leaves
juice of 1 organic orange
juice of ½ organic lemon
1 tsp sugar

1   Few fishmongers are willing to prepare the sardines for you, so this is what you should do. Cut off the heads and the fins (but not the tail), slit the belly and clean out the insides. Lay the sardines on a board, open side down, and press the backbone down gently. Cut the backbone at the tail end and remove it. Wash and dry the fish.

2   Put the currants in a bowl and cover with boiling water. Leave them to plump up for 5–10 minutes. Drain and dry them thoroughly with kitchen paper.

3   Heat 3 tbsp of the oil in a frying pan and fry the breadcrumbs until nicely brown. Mix in the pine nuts, garlic, parsley and currants. Sauté gently for a few minutes and then remove the pan from the heat. Add the cheese and pepper to taste. Taste and add salt if necessary.

4   Heat the oven to 180°C/Gas Mark 4.

5   Sprinkle the sardines on both sides with a little salt and pepper and place them skin side down. Spread a generous teaspoonful of stuffing over each fish and roll up towards the tail. Place them in an oiled baking dish with the tails sticking up in the air.

6   Stick the bay leaves here and there among the little bundles. Drizzle the orange and lemon juices and the rest of the oil all over, then sprinkle with the sugar.

7   Place the dish in the oven and bake for 15 minutes or so. Serve at room temperature.

The combination of sardines and orange is to be found only in Sicily, and this dish produces the best of this unusual yet delicious mixture of flavours. It is an antipasto that is very popular in Palermo and Messina, a peasant dish whose name derives from its appearance. The boned sardines are rolled up around a spoonful of stuffing and set in a dish with their tails in the air, making them look like fat little *beccafichi* – warblers – pecking at the dish.

Sfogi in Saor
SOLE FILLETS IN A SWEET-AND-SOUR SAUCE

Serves 6–8

flour for coating the fish

sea salt

oil for deep frying

700g sole fillets

60g sultanas

2 tbsp olive oil

225g sweet onions, thinly
sliced

2 tsp sugar

120ml good wine vinegar

4 bay leaves

60g pine nuts

2–3 pinches of ground
cinnamon

2 cloves

12 black peppercorns,
lightly bruised

1   Spread some flour on a board and season with salt.

2   Heat oil for deep frying in a wok or a frying pan. Meanwhile, coat the fish lightly in the flour.

3   When the oil is very hot but not smoking (test by frying a small piece of bread: it should brown in 50 seconds), slide in the sole fillets, a few at a time. Fry gently for about 3 minutes on each side until a golden crust has formed. With a fish slice, transfer the fish to a plate lined with kitchen paper to drain.

4   Soak the sultanas in a little warm water to plump them.

5   Heat the olive oil and onions in a small frying pan. Add a pinch of salt and the sugar. Cook the onions gently, stirring frequently, until golden. Turn the heat up and pour in the wine vinegar. Boil briskly until the liquid is reduced by half.

6   Lay the fish neatly in a shallow dish. Pour over the onion sauce and put the bay leaves on top. Drain the sultanas and scatter them on top of the dish together with the pine nuts, spices and peppercorns. Cover the dish with cling film and leave to marinate for 24 hours. If you want to keep the dish for 2 days or more, refrigerate it. Take the dish out of the fridge at least 2 or 3 hours before you want to serve it, so that it has time to reach room temperature.

The taste of this sauce, in which the sole is marinated for 2 days, is strongly reminiscent of Middle Eastern cooking. This is understandable as this is a dish from Venice, a city which in the past had important trade links with the Orient.

Sfogi in saor (Venetian dialect for 'sogliole in sapore', meaning sole in a sauce) is one of the dishes traditionally eaten in Venice during the Feast of the Redeemer, which falls on the third Sunday in July, when the lagoon is lit by thousands of fireworks and carpeted with boats of every size.

Il Mio Carpaccio
MY CARPACCIO

Serves 4

350g fillet of beef
1 egg yolk
180ml extra virgin olive oil
3 tbsp lemon juice
1 tsp Dijon mustard
a few drops of Tabasco sauce
sea salt and freshly ground
 black pepper

1   Put the beef in the freezer for about 3 hours to harden it; this makes it easier to slice thinly.

2   Put the egg yolk in a food processor with 2 tbsp of the oil, the lemon juice, mustard, Tabasco, and some salt and pepper and process for 30 seconds.

3   Add the rest of the oil slowly through the hole in the lid. The sauce will become like a thin mayonnaise. Taste and adjust the seasoning.

4   Remove the beef from the freezer and place on a board. Using an electric carving knife, or a *very* sharp knife, slice it very thinly. Allow the meat to come back to room temperature – about 1 hour.

5   Place the meat neatly on individual plates and pour the sauce over it before serving.

Created by Giuseppe Cipriani at Harry's Bar for one of his clients who was on a strict diet, carpaccio has now become the byword for any fish or meat served raw and dressed with some sort of olive-oil-based sauce. Each cook varies the sauce according to his or her preference, so you can experiment with your carpaccio. This is my version.

I use an electric carving knife to slice the beef very thinly, but if you do not have one, carve the meat then put the slices between 2 sheets of cling film and beat with a rolling pin to make them thinner.

OTHER FAVOURITES

The title of this section is self-explanatory. These are recipes I wanted to include, but which did not fit into any of the other categories.

Radicchio Rosso e Cicoria Belga Alla Trevisana
GRILLED RADICCHIO AND CHICORY

Serves 6

450g red radicchio
225g chicory
6 tbsp extra virgin olive oil
sea salt and freshly ground
 black pepper

1   Heat the grill.
2   Wash the radicchio and chicory carefully. Dry thoroughly. Cut the radicchio into quarters and the chicory in half, both lengthways.
3   Place the radicchio and chicory in the grill pan (or on a hot griddle). Spoon over the oil and season with salt and a generous amount of pepper.
4   Cook under the grill (or on the griddle) for 10 minutes, taking care to turn the heat down if the vegetables start to burn. Turn the pieces over halfway through the cooking. The vegetables are ready when the thick core can be pierced easily.
5   Transfer the grilled vegetables to a dish and spoon over the juice from the grill pan. Serve hot or cold.

The radicchio rosso used in Veneto for this dish is the long radicchio of Treviso, which can now sometimes be found in specialist greengrocers during the autumn. It has the characteristic bitterness of radicchio, delicate yet more pronounced than the round Rosa di Chioggia, which is the kind of radicchio available everywhere all year round. The Rosa di Chioggia is a modern type of radicchio which is grown in greenhouses. It is tougher in texture and blander in flavour, with a similarity to white cabbage. However, the use of heat in this recipe brings out the flavour. Chicory is very good prepared in this way.

Cipolline Brasate
BRAISED BABY ONIONS

These onions, served cold, often form part of a spectacular Piedmontese antipasto. They can also accompany cold meat or, served hot, boiled or braised meat dishes. The onions used in Italy are the white, squat kind, very sweet in taste. Unfortunately they are not easily available outside Italy, but you can use small young pickling onions instead.

Serves 4

700g small onions
4 tbsp olive oil
15g butter
2 tsp tomato purée dissolved
  in 150ml pint hot water
2 tbsp sugar
2 tbsp red wine vinegar
sea salt and freshly ground
  black pepper

1   Put the onions in a pan of boiling water. Bring back to the boil and blanch for 1 minute. Drain and remove the outside skin, taking care to remove only the dangling roots and not the base of the root, otherwise the onions will come apart during the cooking.
2   Choose a large sauté pan and put in the onions, olive oil and butter. Sauté the onions until golden, shaking the pan often.
3   Add the diluted tomato purée, sugar, vinegar, and salt and pepper to taste. Cook, uncovered, for about 1 hour, adding a little more water if necessary. The onions are ready when they are a rich brown colour and can easily be pierced by a fork. Serve hot or cold, but not chilled.

Frittelle di Mozzarella
MOZZARELLA AND PARMESAN FRITTERS

Serves 4

225g Italian mozzarella
1 large egg
75g Parmesan, freshly grated
2 tbsp flour
12 fresh basil leaves
1 small garlic clove, finely
 chopped
sea salt and freshly ground
 black pepper
oil for deep frying

The mozzarella in this dish must be drained of its liquid for 24 hours to allow it to dry out.

1 Grate the mozzarella through the largest holes of a cheese grater and put it in a bowl.

2 Beat the egg lightly and add to the bowl with the Parmesan and flour.

3 Wipe the basil leaves with damp kitchen paper and snip them with scissors. Mix into the mozzarella mixture with the garlic, a generous grinding of pepper and a little salt. (Add salt with caution because the Parmesan is salty.) Mix thoroughly.

4 With damp hands, shape the mixture into small balls, the size of a walnut. If the mixture is too sloppy add a little more flour. Put the balls on a wooden board and chill for at least 30 minutes.

5 Heat oil in a wok or a small deep saucepan. When the oil is very hot but not yet smoking (the right temperature is 180°C, i.e. when a small piece of bread will turn golden in 50 seconds) slide in the cheese balls. Do not crowd the pan or they will not fry properly. Turn them over and when they are deep gold all over, fish them out with a slotted spoon and put them on kitchen paper to drain. Serve hot.

Carote in Agrodolce
CARROTS IN A WINE AND HERB SAUCE

Serves 6

900g carrots
6 tbsp olive oil
250ml dry white wine
120ml white wine vinegar
2 sprigs of fresh flat-leaf
  parsley
2 springs of fresh thyme
4 fresh sage leaves
2 bay leaves
4 springs of fresh mint
2 garlic cloves, cut in half
sea salt and freshly ground
  black pepper
2 tbsp sugar

1 Cut the carrots into thick matchsticks and put them in a sauté pan.
2 Add all the other ingredients plus 250ml of water. Bring to the boil and cook, uncovered, for 30 minutes. The carrots will still be quite crunchy.
3 Lift the carrots out of the pan with a slotted spoon and put them to one side in a bowl.
4 Boil the liquid rapidly to reduce until it is very tasty and of a beautiful deep gold colour. Most of the water will have evaporated and you will be left with a delicious hot herby vinaigrette. Taste and adjust the seasoning.
5 Pour the reduced liquid over the carrots and leave to marinate for 48 hours.
6 Remove the herbs and garlic before serving.

Carrots, which in Britain are very good, are underrated vegetables. In this sweet-and-sour sauce they become an ideal autumn or winter antipasto.

Caponata

AUBERGINE, ONION AND CELERY STEW

Serves 4

700g aubergines
vegetable oil for frying
sea salt and freshly ground
 black pepper
the inner sticks of 1 celery
 head, coarse threads removed
100ml olive oil
1 onion, very finely sliced
225g Italian canned plum
 tomatoes, chopped
1 tbsp sugar
90ml white wine vinegar
1 tbsp grated bitter chocolate
 (70% cocoa solids)
60g capers
60g large green olives, stoned
 and quartered
2 hard-boiled eggs

1   Cut the aubergines into pieces. Heat 2.5cm of vegetable oil in a frying pan. When the oil is hot (it is ready when it sizzles around a cube of aubergine) add a layer of aubergines and fry until golden brown on all sides. Drain on kitchen paper. Repeat until all the aubergines are cooked. Season each batch lightly with salt.

2   Cut the celery into pieces the same size as the aubergine. Fry it in the same oil until golden and crisp. Drain on kitchen paper.

3   Pour the olive oil into a clean frying pan and add the onion. Sauté gently for about 10 minutes until soft. Add the tomatoes and cook, stirring frequently, over a moderate heat for about 15 minutes. Season with salt and pepper.

4   While the sauce is cooking, heat the sugar and vinegar in a small saucepan. Add the chocolate, capers and olives and cook gently until the chocolate has melted. Add to the tomato sauce and cook for 5 minutes.

5   Mix the aubergines and celery into the tomato sauce. Stir and cook for 20 minutes so that the flavours of the ingredients can blend together. Pour the caponata into a serving dish and allow to cool.

6   Pass the hard-boiled eggs through the smallest holes of a food mill, or push through a metal sieve. Before serving, cover the caponata with the sieved eggs.

Thanks to the creativity of the Sicilians, the humble aubergine here forms the basis of one of the grandest vegetable dishes. Caponata appears in many different versions throughout the island. It can be garnished with tiny boiled octopus, a small lobster, prawns or *bottarga* – the air-dried roe of the grey mullet, a speciality of Sardinia. I garnish this one with hard-boiled eggs, thus making it a perfect vegetarian dish. The secret of a good caponata is that the three vegetables, aubergine, celery and onion, must be cooked separately and only after cooking combined together and added to the other ingredients. Caponata is best made at least 24 hours in advance.

Bagna Caôda
HOT GARLICKY DIP FOR RAW VEGETABLES

Serves 4–6

assortment of raw vegetables
  such as cardoons, celery,
  cauliflower, courgettes,
  carrots, radishes and peppers
75g unsalted butter
5 garlic cloves, very finely
  sliced or chopped
60g salted anchovies, boned,
  rinsed and chopped, or
  canned anchovy fillets,
  chopped
150ml extra virgin olive oil
sea salt

1   First prepare the vegetables. Cardoons are the traditional vegetable for bagna caôda, but they are not easy to find in Britain. If you find some, they will usually have already had their outer leaves and tough stalks removed. You will have to remove the strings, as you do with celery sticks. Cut the stalks and the heart into suitable pieces. Rub any cut part with lemon to prevent discolouring. Prepare all the other vegetables as you do for a normal dip, i.e. washing, scraping, stringing, according to the vegetable, and then cutting into fingers. Choose the best specimens and discard any bruised parts.

2   Melt the butter in a small, deep earthenware pot or a very heavy-bottomed saucepan over the lowest heat. As soon as the butter has melted and begun to foam, add the garlic and cook for a minute or so. The garlic should not colour. Add the anchovies to the pot and pour in the oil very gradually, stirring the whole time. Cook for about 10 minutes, always on the lowest possible heat and stirring constantly. The sauce should never come near to boiling point. The dip is ready when the anchovies have become a paste. Taste and add salt if necessary. Pepper is not added to traditional bagna caôda.

3   Bring the pot to the table together with the prepared vegetables, and place it over a low flame or on a table heater.

Bagna caôda is a peasant dish from Piedmont, where it is made in earthenware pots kept hot on glowing embers. A small deep earthenware pot is by far the best receptacle in which to make it. You will also need a table heater or candle burner in the middle of the table to keep the bagna caôda hot, though it must not cook. The vegetables are dipped, raw, into the sauce, although some cooks prefer to blanch the cardoons and celeriac. Plenty of crusty bread and full-bodied red wine, such as a Dolcetto, Barolo or Nebbiolo, are the other essentials. The oil used should be a mild extra virgin one from Liguria, not a peppery oil from Tuscany.

Uova Soda alla Pugliese con i Pomodori Secchi

HARD-BOILED EGGS WITH PARSLEY AND BREADCRUMB TOPPING & SUN-DRIED TOMATOES

Serves 4

250g sun-dried tomatoes
 in olive oil
6 large eggs
100ml extra virgin olive oil
6 tbsp dried white breadcrumbs
2 tbsp good red wine vinegar,
 but not balsamic vinegar
3 garlic cloves, chopped
6 tbsp chopped flat-leaf
 parsley
2–3 dried chillies, according
 to taste, chopped
sea salt and freshly ground
 black pepper

1   Drain the tomatoes of their preserving oil and set aside while you prepare the eggs.

2   Hard-boil the eggs: lower them into a pan of simmering water and cook for 8 minutes, no longer, so that the yolks will be just hard. Put the saucepan under cold running water and leave for 1 minute. Crack the shells all round and peel them off. Leave the eggs to cool right through in the cold water while you make the topping.

3   Heat 3 tbsp of the oil in a small frying pan. Add the breadcrumbs and sauté for a couple of minutes, stirring constantly, until the crumbs are golden. Add 1 tbsp of the remaining oil to the pan with the vinegar and all the other ingredients. Sauté gently for a further couple of minutes. Taste and adjust the seasoning.

4   Drain and dry the eggs. Cut them in half lengthways. To prevent the egg halves sliding on the dish, slice off a tiny bit of the white on the round side, to give a flat base. Arrange the eggs on a serving dish and drizzle with the remaining oil. Season lightly with salt and pepper and pile about 2 tsp of the topping over each egg half. Surround with the tomatoes drained of their oil.

These eggs are served at room temperature. I like to surround them with charred and peeled yellow and red peppers (page 35), or, as here, with sun-dried tomatoes generously dressed with extra virgin olive oil and seasoned with garlic, salt and pepper. I also scatter black olives here and there round the dish.

'I like all simple things, boiled eggs, oysters
and caviar, *truite au bleu*, grilled salmon,
roast lamb (the saddle by preference),
cold grouse, treacle tart and rice pudding.
But of all simple things the only one I can eat
day in and day out, not only without disgust
but with the eagerness of an appetite
unimpaired by excess, is macaroni.'

From a short story, 'The Hairless Mexican' by
W. SOMERSET MAUGHAM

PASTA

Pasta is the simplest food, even simpler than bread, consisting only of semolina and water for dried pasta and flour and eggs for home-made pasta. It is also the food that can change its character and appearance more than any other, like some great character actor assuming countless different roles. Think of the golden lightness of a delicate dish of tagliatelle with butter and compare it with the intriguing, exotic flavour of a green dish of spaghetti with pesto, or the rich earthiness of a baked lasagne. All are equally good in their different ways, and pasta is the main ingredient of them all.

TYPES OF PASTA

We Italians never look down on **dried pasta**. We consider it ideal for many sauces and would never regard it as merely a substitute for home-made pasta. Factory-made dried pasta is made from durum wheat ground into semolina and mixed to a paste with water. The dough is forced through perforated metal discs to form the desired shape, and then dried. It should be buff-yellow, translucent and slightly shiny. The most common kinds are long pasta of various widths and lengths such as spaghetti, shapes such as fusilli, penne and conchiglie, lasagne and small pasta for soups.

The '**fresh pasta**' sold in delicatessens or supermarkets is made with durum wheat semolina, flour, eggs and water. Though it is convenient, it certainly is not as good as home-made pasta, and it compares badly with dried pasta of a good Italian brand.

Home-made pasta has a lightness and delicacy that shop-bought 'fresh pasta' cannot match. So, when you want to make a recipe that calls for fresh pasta, do try to make it yourself, whether by hand or with the help of a machine. Remember, though, that it is not easy to make pasta by hand without practice, time and a long, thin pasta rolling pin.

Luckily there are good machines to speed up the task. Some electric machines make good pasta, but they are expensive, noisy and difficult to clean. The hand-cranked machines are cheap and easily obtained.

THE COOKING OF PASTA

It is easy to cook pasta, but it can be spoiled by carelessness. Pasta needs to be cooked in a large saucepan and a lot of salted water – about 1 litre for 100g of pasta. Bring the water to the boil and then add cooking salt – about 1½ tbsp for 4 litres, which is the quantity needed for 300–500g of pasta.

Slide all the pasta into the boiling water, stir with a wooden fork or spoon to separate the pasta shapes, and cover the pan so that the water returns to the boil as soon as possible. Remove the lid and adjust the heat so that the water boils briskly, but does not boil over. The pasta is ready when it is al dente, which means that it offers some resistance to the bite. The best test to see if the pasta is ready is to fish out a piece and pop it in your mouth. It is absolutely unnecessary to add cold water to pasta after cooking, as is sometimes suggested by non-Italian cookery writers.

The time pasta takes to cook differs according to its quality and shape, whether it is fresh or dried, and, of course, personal preference. Even in Italy a plate of spaghetti that would be perfect in Naples might be considered undercooked in Milan.

So I suggest for shop-bought dried pasta you follow the manufacturer's instructions, tasting the pasta about 1 minute before the end of the cooking time, so that you can decide for yourself when it is ready.

As for fresh home-made pasta, remember that it takes far less time to cook than dried pasta. Tagliatelle cook in 2–3 minutes and stuffed pasta in 4–5 minutes. This timing is calculated after the water returns to the boil.

THE AGNESI METHOD

This method of cooking factory-dried pasta was shown to me by the late Vincenzo Agnesi. I use it when I have friends to dinner since the pasta does not overcook if you leave it a minute too long in the pot. It also retains the characteristic flavour of semolina.

Bring a large saucepan of water to the boil, add sea salt to taste, then the pasta and stir. When the water has come back to the boil, cook for 1 minute, stirring frequently. Turn off the heat, put a tea towel over the pan and close with a tight-fitting lid. Leave for the same length of time that the pasta would take to cook by the normal method, i.e. if it were still boiling, then drain and serve.

DRAINING PASTA

Pasta should be drained as soon as it is al dente (literally, 'to the tooth'): you must be able to feel its texture when you bite into it. However, if the pasta is going to be cooked further, by baking or frying, drain it when it is still slightly undercooked. Pasta for salads should be even more al dente.

It is important to drain pasta properly. Use a colander that is large enough to contain all the pasta and that has feet to stand on. Tip in the pasta, give the colander two sharp shakes, and immediately turn the pasta into a heated bowl, the frying pan with the sauce or the saucepan in which it was cooked. (It's easier to toss it in the pan without making a mess.) Gnocchi and hollow shapes need more draining because water may be trapped. However, pasta should never be overdrained, as it needs to be slippery for coating with the sauce.

Do not leave it sitting 'naked' in the colander. It should be dressed as soon as it is drained.

In southern Italy they do not use a colander for long pasta. The spaghetti is lifted out of the pan with two long forks. It is kept in the air for a few seconds for the excess water to run off and then immediately transferred to the pan or serving bowl. The Neapolitans say 'Gli spaghetti devono avere la goccia' – spaghetti must be still just dripping.

Home-made Pasta
MAKING THE DOUGH

about 200g Italian 00 flour
semolina for dusting
2 large eggs

*Makes about 350g pasta,
enough for 4 people as a first
course or 3 as a main course*

Note: I recommend the use of Italian Grade 00 flour for making pasta dough. It is the best for this purpose because it absorbs the eggs more evenly, is easier to knead and roll out and, above all, makes pasta of a more fragrant flavour and a more delicate texture. Italian 00 flour is now available in most supermarkets and delicatessens.

1   Put most of the flour on the work surface and make a well in the centre. Place the rest of the flour to one side. Break the eggs into the well. Beat them lightly with a fork for about 1 minute, then draw the flour in gradually from the inner wall of the well. I do this with 2 fingers because I find that gives me more control. When the eggs are no longer runny draw in enough flour to enable you to knead the dough. At this stage you might have to add the flour you set aside, and even a little more from the bag, which you should keep at hand. You should add enough flour so that the dough is no longer sticky. (It is not possible to give the exact amount of flour needed because it depends on the absorption capacity of the eggs and the humidity of the kitchen.) Work until the flour and eggs are thoroughly amalgamated, put the dough to one side and scrape the work surface clean. Wash and dry your hands.

Note: It is easier for a beginner to stretch a soft dough, though a dough that is too soft may stick and tear and become unmanageable. You can make a harder dough by replacing half the flour with fine semolina. This dough is difficult to work by hand, but it can be rolled out using the hand-cranked machine. It makes a pasta that is less delicate and less smooth in texture, but with a definite flavour, particularly suitable for vegetable sauces.

2   Proceed to knead the dough by pressing and pushing with the heel of your palm, folding the dough back, giving it half a turn and repeating these movements. Repeat the movements for about 10 minutes if you are going to make your pasta by hand, or 2–3 minutes if you are going to use a machine. Wrap the dough in cling film and leave it to rest for at least 30 minutes, though you can leave it for up to 3 hours, or even overnight.

ROLLING OUT BY HAND

To roll out by hand you ideally need a *mattarello* – a long, thin Italian rolling pin – which is about 82cm long and 3.7cm in diameter. If you do not have one you must divide the dough and roll it out in 2 batches so that the circle of pasta does not become too large for your pin.

ROLLING OUT BY MACHINE

I still think the hand-cranked machine is the best machine to use, and worth every penny of its very reasonable price. This is how to proceed. Lightly dust the work surface with flour. Unwrap the dough and knead, as before, for a further 2 minutes, then divide it into 4 equal parts. Take one piece of dough and carefully rewrap the others in cling film.
Set the rollers of the machine to the widest opening. Flatten the piece of dough slightly, so that it nearly reaches the width of the machine. Run it through 5 or 6 times, folding the sheet over and giving it a 180° turn each time. When the dough is smooth, run the sheet, unfolded and without turning it, through all the settings, closing the rollers one notch at a time until you achieve the desired thickness. For good results it is very important that you push the sheet of dough through each setting. If the sheet tears or sticks to the machine, dust it on both sides with flour. For tonnarelli (like spaghetti but square in section) stop the rolling out at the second-from-last setting. For tagliatelle or tagliolini stop at the last but one. For flat sheet pasta stop at the last setting.
If the atmosphere is damp, dough rolled out too thin cannot be stuffed to make ravioli or other small shapes as, instead of drying, it becomes more and more soggy when filled with the stuffing. If you find this happening, stop rolling out at the last but one setting. Alternatively, I sometimes prefer to roll out the strip twice through the last but one setting. This makes the pasta just a little thinner, but not as thin as the last setting. Roll out the dough to the last setting only for lasagne or cannelloni.

LONG PASTA, TAGLIATELLE, FETTUCCINE, TONNARELLI, TAGLIOLINI

Lay each sheet of dough on a clean tea towel, letting about one-third of its length hang down over the edge of the work surface. Leave until the pasta is dry to the touch and slightly leathery, but still pliable.

This process takes about 30 minutes depending on the humidity of the atmosphere and texture of the pasta, and is essential because it prevents the strands sticking together. Feed each sheet through the broad cutters of the machine for tagliatelle or fettuccine, or through the narrow ones for tonnarelli or tagliolini.

Separate the cut strands or wind them loosely round your hand to make nests. Spread them out on clean tea towels, and lightly dust them with semolina. Do not use flour, as this would be absorbed into the dough. The pasta is now ready to be cooked, or it can be dried and then stored in an airtight tin or plastic bag. Be very careful how you handle it because dried home-made pasta is very brittle and breaks easily.

LASAGNE AND CANNELLONI

Proceed immediately to cut the shapes without drying the sheets. Cut each pasta sheet into squares of about 12 x 8.5cm for lasagne, or 10 x 7.5cm for cannelloni.

PAPPARDELLE

Roll out each sheet of pasta to the last but one notch of the hand-cranked machine. Leave to dry for no more than 10 minutes and then cut into ribbons about 12–15cm long and 1.5cm wide. Lay the pappardelle, not touching each other, on clean tea towels.

STUFFED PASTA SHAPES

You must work straight away while the pasta dough is still fresh and pliable. Roll out the dough and stuff the sheets, one or two at a time, depending on the shape. Keep the remainder of the dough in cling film.
Cook the little shapes straight away or leave them until the next day, spread out on a clean cloth, dusted with semolina. Once dry, you can store stuffed pasta in plastic boxes, in layers interleaved with greaseproof paper. Do not keep them for longer than a day or the stuffing might be spoiled.

Green Pasta

150g cooked fresh spinach, or frozen spinach, thawed and cooked for 5 minutes
225g Italian 00 flour
2 large eggs

Note: The only coloured pasta I consider worth writing about is the traditional green pasta made with spinach. All the modern red, black or brown pasta are gimmicks, and sometimes they spoil the flavour of the pasta. Flavour and colour should be added only by the sauce.
1 Squeeze all the liquid out of the spinach with your hands. Chop it very finely with a knife. Do not use a food processor as the spinach would become like a liquid mass. Add the chopped spinach to the well in the flour together with the eggs, and knead and roll out as for normal pasta.

SAUCES FOR SHAPES

In Italy there are said to be 350 different shapes of pasta (I've never counted them!). Although you are unlikely to find such a vast number of pasta shapes outside Italy, there are now a very considerable number to choose from. In the recipes I explain which shape of pasta is usually dressed with the sauce in question, but you do not have to follow my suggestions slavishly. There are, however, certain basic rules that govern which pasta shapes should be dressed with which sauce. In general, long thin shapes are dressed with an olive oil-based sauce that allows the strands to remain slippery and separate. A typical recipe is the spaghettini with oil, garlic and chilli on page 98.

Thicker long shapes, such as ziti, tonnarelli, bucatini or fettuccine, are best in heavier sauces containing prosciutto or bits of meat, cheese and eggs. A prime example is the carbonara on page 123.

Medium-size short tubular pasta like ditali, orecchiette and fusilli are perfect with vegetable sauces of any kind, these being the shapes traditionally made in southern Italy where pasta is most often combined with vegetables. See recipe for the orecchiette with broccoli on page 103.

Penne and maccheroni and other large tubular shapes, as well as home-made shapes such as garganelli and pappardelle, are the perfect foil for a rich meat *ragù* and for use in most baked dishes. A *ragù* bolognese is traditionally combined with tagliatelle (see page 112), and the choice for a northern Italian pasta al gratin (page 137) is penne.

As for the proportion of sauce to pasta, an average of 2 generous tbsp of well-reduced sauce per portion of pasta is a good general guide.

ARRANGEMENT OF RECIPES

The recipes in this book are grouped according to the main ingredient of the sauce. Thus tagliatelle with bolognese sauce will be found with other recipes whose sauces are based on fish and meat products, while spaghetti with tomato sauce is with the other recipes for vegetable-based sauces.

PASTA WITH VEGETABLE SAUCES

Pesto
PESTO SAUCE

30g pine nuts
90g fresh basil leaves
1 garlic clove, peeled
pinch of sea salt
4 level tbsp freshly grated
 Parmesan
2 level tbsp freshly grated
 aged pecorino
90ml extra virgin olive oil
40g unsalted butter

*Pesto freezes very well. Omit
the garlic and the cheeses and
add them just before you are
going to use the sauce.*

1 Heat the oven to 180°C/Gas Mark 4. Spread the pine nuts on a baking tray and toast in the oven for 5 minutes or so. This will bring out the flavour of the nuts.

2 To make in a mortar: Put the basil leaves, garlic, pine nuts and salt in the mortar. Grind against the sides of the mortar with the pestle, crushing the ingredients until the mixture has become a paste. Mix in the grated cheeses. Add the oil gradually, beating with a wooden spoon.

To make in a food processor or blender: Cut the garlic into thin slices and drop them into the container of the food processor or blender. Add the basil, pine nuts, salt and oil and process to a creamy consistency. Transfer the sauce to a bowl and mix in the cheeses.

3 Melt the butter over the lowest heat and blend into the pesto.

Use young basil leaves for pesto; basil that has been growing for too long acquires an unpleasantly strong taste. The pine nuts must be fresh, i.e. of the current year, and the oil must be a very good olive oil, although an unassertive one. If possible use an oil from Liguria or Lake Garda; they are less pungent than a Tuscan oil, and less herby than an oil from Puglia.

The oil must be added slowly, as for mayonnaise, so as to create the right thickness. Some cooks add walnuts as well as pine nuts, but I prefer to add only pine nuts in order to keep the emphasis on the fresh flavour of the basil. If you have time, make your pesto by hand in a mortar; more juices are released than would be by the chopping action of the metal blade in a food processor or blender. I add a little softened butter to the pesto just before serving, to make the sauce sweeter and more delicate. Before tossing the pesto with the pasta, always dilute it with 3 or 4 tbsp of the water in which the pasta has been cooking.

Trofie al Pesto
TROFIE WITH PESTO SAUCE

Serves 4 as a main course

3 small new potatoes
225g young French beans
400g dried trofie
pesto sauce from the previous
 recipe

1   Cook the potatoes in their skins in boiling salted water. Drain, then peel and slice them. Put in a bowl.

2   Top and tail the beans. Cook them in plenty of boiling salted water until tender and then drain. Add to the potatoes. Toss with 3 or 4 tbsp of the pesto.

3   Cook the pasta in plenty of boiling salted water until al dente. Drain, reserving a cupful of the water, and return to the pan. Add 2 or 3 tbsp of the water to the pesto.

4   Toss the pasta with half the pesto. Transfer half the pasta to a serving dish. Spoon the potato and bean mixture over the pasta and cover with the rest of the pasta. Spread the remaining pesto over the top.

In Liguria, the motherland of pesto, potato and a handful of French beans are cooked with the pasta. The pasta I like to use in this recipe is trofie, a shape traditionally served with pesto in Genoa. If you cannot find it, use fusilli.

Penne in Salsa di Cipolle
PENNE WITH ONION SAUCE

Serves 4 as a starter
or 3 as a main course

4 tbsp olive oil
500g red onions, very finely
 sliced
sea salt and freshly ground
 black pepper
½ tsp Marmite
1 tsp plain flour
350g penne
25g unsalted butter
freshly grated Parmigiano-
 Reggiano

1 Put the oil and the onion in a large sauté pan (one that has a lid), sprinkle with salt and cook for 10 minutes over a very low heat, stirring very often. Stir in the Marmite, cook for 1 minute and then mix in the flour. Mix thoroughly to incorporate the flour. Add about 100ml of boiling water and mix until all the liquid is simmering. Put the lid on the pan and cook over a very low heat for 30 minutes or so, stirring often and adding a few tablespoons of hot water whenever the onion starts to become too dry.

2 Cook the penne in plenty of salted boiling water until al dente and, when it's ready, drain it and then add to the onion sauce. Stir-fry for a minute or two, then turn off the heat and mix in the butter. Mix well until the butter has melted and then serve, handing round the cheese in a bowl.

This is my standby sauce for pasta during the winter when I find tomato sauce too summery and cool, and comforting enough on a dark cold day.

Pasta al Sugo
PASTA WITH TOMATO SAUCE *(Version 1)*

Serves 6 as a first course
or 4 as a main course

1 medium-sized onion,
 very finely chopped
1 medium-sized carrot,
 very finely chopped
1 celery stick, very finely
 chopped
4 tbsp olive oil
1 garlic clove, very finely
 chopped
1 small dried chilli, seeded
 and chopped (optional)
800g Italian canned plum
 tomatoes, coarsely chopped
4 parsley stalks
1 bay leaf
1 tsp dried oregano
1 tsp sugar
sea salt and freshly ground
 black pepper
500g bucatini or spaghetti
freshly grated Parmesan,
 to serve

The first tomato sauce here is denser and darker than the second one because of the many sautéed vegetables. I like it best for dressing a dish of penne or bucatini, although it is suitable for most dried pasta.

1 Sauté slowly the onion, carrot and celery in the olive oil until well softened (at least 10 minutes). Add the garlic and chilli just a few minutes before you finish the *soffritto* (sautéed mixture).
2 Add the chopped tomatoes, the herbs and sugar. Season lightly with salt and pepper.
3 Allow to simmer gently, uncovered, for 30–40 minutes, until the oil begins to separate out into small drops around the edge. Stir occasionally to prevent the sauce sticking to the bottom.
4 Remove and discard the parsley stalks and the bay leaf. Push the sauce through the coarsest disc of a mouli legume, or blitz it for a few seconds in a food processor – or leave it as it is, as I often do. Spoon the sauce back into the saucepan and keep it hot while you cook the pasta.
5 Cook the pasta in plenty of boiling salted water until al dente. Drain well and toss with the sauce. Serve at once, and hand round a bowl of freshly grated Parmesan.

Tomato Sauce *(Version 2)*
A simpler and fresher tomato sauce can be made in the summer when good fresh tomatoes are on the market. Peel, seed and coarsely chop 900g of ripe tomatoes and put them in a large heavy-bottomed sauté pan with 5 tbsp extra virgin olive oil, 6 bruised garlic cloves, salt and freshly ground black pepper, a dozen snipped fresh basil leaves or ½ tbsp of dried oregano. Cook briskly for 5 minutes, stirring frequently, until a lot of the tomato water has evaporated. Remove and discard the garlic before serving. This is the classic sauce for spaghetti.

Spaghettini Aglio Olio e Peperoncino
SPAGHETTINI WITH OIL, GARLIC AND CHILLI

Serves 4 as a first course
or 3 as a main course

350g spaghettini (thin
 spaghetti)
sea salt
120ml extra virgin olive oil
3 garlic cloves, sliced
1 or 2 dried chillies, according
 to taste, seeded and crumbled

*No cheese is needed for this
typically Neapolitan quick
pasta.*

1   Cook the pasta in plenty of boiling salted water, remembering that spaghettini will cook in about 6 minutes.
2   Meanwhile, put the oil, garlic and chillies in a frying pan large enough to hold all the pasta later. Cook for 1 minute over a low heat. As soon as the garlic aroma rises, the sauce is ready. Draw off the heat immediately or the garlic might burn; this would ruin the taste of the oil.
3   Drain the pasta as soon as it is al dente. Do not overcook it. Transfer the pasta immediately to the frying pan. Stir-fry for a minute or so, using 2 forks and lifting the spaghetti high into the air so that every strand is beautifully glistening with oil. Serve at once, preferably straight from the pan.

This sauce differs from that in Tagliatelle with Butter and Parmesan (page 139), in a way that demonstrates the essential difference between the cooking of northern Italy and that of the South. The aggressive flavour of this dish shows all the characteristics of Mediterranean cooking, while the delicate, but certainly not bland, Tagliatelle with Butter epitomises northern Italian cooking with its abundant use of butter and Parmesan.

Paparele e Bisi
TAGLIATELLE WITH PEAS

Serves 6 as a first course
or 4 as a main course

60g butter
60g unsmoked pancetta,
 chopped
1 tbsp finely chopped onion
300g cooked peas, or frozen
 petits pois, thawed
1 tbsp chopped flat-leaf
 parsley
120ml chicken stock
sea salt and freshly ground
 black pepper
home-made tagliatelle made
 with 3 large eggs and
 300g Italian 00 flour,
 or 450g Italian dried egg
 tagliatelle
60g Parmesan, freshly grated

1   Put half the butter, the pancetta and the onion in a small saucepan and sauté until the onion is soft and golden.

2   Mix in the peas and the parsley and then pour over the stock. Stir and add salt and pepper to taste. Cover the pan and cook over gentle heat until the peas are tender. The sauce should be quite thin.

3   Meanwhile, cook the pasta in plenty of boiling salted water until it is al dente. Drain and return to the pan.

4   Toss the pasta with the rest of the butter, pour the sauce over the top and mix in the Parmesan.

'Paparele' and 'bisi' are the Venetian words for wide tagliatelle and *piselli*, peas, which are one of the Venetians' favourite vegetables. Here they are used to dress fresh tagliatelle in a delicate, well-balanced sauce. The sauce is also suitable for dressing a dish of dried farfalle.

Orecchiette con i Broccoli
PASTA WITH BROCCOLI

Serves 4 as a first course
or 3 as a main course

450g broccoli
sea salt and freshly ground
  black pepper
350g orecchiette or other
  medium-sized pasta, or
  350g wholemeal spaghetti
2 garlic cloves, peeled
1 dried chilli, seeded
3 salted anchovies, boned and
  rinsed, or 6 canned anchovy
  fillets, drained
6 tbsp extra virgin olive oil
4 tbsp freshly grated aged
  pecorino

1 Trim the broccoli. Divide into small florets and cut the stalks into 2.5cm rounds.
2 Bring a large saucepan of water to the boil. Add about 1½ tbsp of cooking salt and then slide in the broccoli. Stir well and cook for 5 minutes after the water has come back to the boil. Retrieve the broccoli from the water with a slotted spoon and lay them on kitchen paper. Pat dry and set aside.
3 Bring the broccoli water back to the boil and add the pasta. Cook in the usual way until very al dente.
4 While the pasta is cooking, chop the garlic, chilli and anchovy fillets together and sauté them in half the oil for 2 minutes, using a large frying pan. Mix in the broccoli and sauté for a few minutes, turning constantly.
5 When the pasta is done, drain and turn it into the frying pan. Stir-fry for 1 minute, then taste and check the seasoning.
6 Before you serve the pasta, pour over the rest of the olive oil and mix in the pecorino. If you like you can serve a bowl of freshly grated Parmesan on the side, although I find that the pecorino gives the dish enough of a cheesy taste.

The combination of vegetables and pasta has its origins in southern Italy. In Puglia this sauce is always served with orecchiette, which means 'little ears' because of their hollow shape. Orecchiette are made at home there, with semolina, flour and water, and they are now produced commercially by the best Italian pasta manufacturers.

I find that this sauce, as well as being good with orecchiette, is also one of the few that can stand up to the nutty flavour of brown pasta made with wholemeal flour (a flavour of which, like most Italians, I am not particularly fond). Wholemeal pasta is made in a number of shapes, among which spaghetti is by far the most successful.

Tagliatelle col Sugo di Funghi
TAGLIATELLE WITH MUSHROOM SAUCE

Serves 6 as a first course
or 4 as a main course

30g dried porcini
450g mixed fresh mushrooms:
 cultivated mushrooms,
 chestnut mushrooms,
 oyster mushrooms,
 brown mushrooms
 (champignons de Paris)
75g unsalted butter
4 shallots, very finely chopped
sea salt and freshly ground
 black pepper
1 garlic clove, finely chopped
1 tbsp chopped flat-leaf parsley
1 tbsp chopped fresh marjoram,
 or 2 tsp dried marjoram
2 tsp tomato purée
1 tbsp plain flour
 or Italian 00 flour
225ml chicken stock
150ml dry white wine
about ¼ of a nutmeg, grated
home-made tagliatelle, made
 with 3 large eggs and
 300g Italian 00 flour
 (page 85), or 450g Italian
 dried egg tagliatelle
freshly grated Parmesan,
 to serve (optional)

I have adapted an old family recipe to suit the mushrooms that are available in Britain. Admittedly there are more and more species of wild mushrooms in the shops these days, especially during the autumn months, the mushroom season, but they are not equally available in all parts of the country. The other reason why I have adapted the Italian recipe is that the sauce is so good that I want to be able to make it at any time of the year, and not only when the wild mushrooms are in season.

The woody, leafy perfume of ceps is given here by the dried porcini, which you can easily buy in Italian delicatessens and many supermarkets. To these you add a selection of cultivated mushrooms for a sweeter flavour and for texture.

1 Put the dried porcini in a bowl and cover with very hot water. Set aside to soak for 30 minutes or so and then lift them out. If they still have some grit, rinse under cold water. Pat the porcini dry and chop them. Filter the liquid through a muslin-lined sieve and reserve.

2 Clean the fresh mushrooms by wiping them with damp kitchen paper. If they are very dirty, rinse them under cold water. Dry and chop them coarsely. (I use a food processor, which I pulsate for only a few seconds.)

Recipe continued overleaf

TAGLIATELLE WITH MUSHROOM SAUCE

continued

3 Put half the butter and the shallots in a large sauté pan, add a pinch of salt and cook until the shallots are soft. Stir in the garlic and the herbs and sauté for a further minute. Add the tomato purée and cook for 30 seconds. Add the dried porcini, sauté for 5 minutes and then add the fresh mushrooms. Sauté over a moderate heat for 5 minutes, turning the mushrooms over and over to *insaporire* – take up the flavour. Season with a little more salt and with a generous grinding of pepper. Turn the heat down and cook for a further 5 minutes.

4 Melt the remaining butter in a heavy saucepan and blend in the flour. Add the stock, stirring constantly and hard until well blended.

5 Heat the wine and add to the butter and stock mixture together with the nutmeg. Add some of the filtered porcini liquid, just enough to add mushroom flavour to the sauce, but not too much because it can be overpowering. Continue cooking very gently for about 15 minutes. Stir in the mushroom mixture. Check the seasoning and cook over the lowest possible heat for about 10 minutes.

6 Meanwhile, cook the tagliatelle in plenty of boiling salted water until al dente. Drain, but do not overdrain, reserving a cupful of the water.

7 Turn half the pasta into a heated bowl and toss with half the mushroom sauce. Cover with the rest of the pasta and mix in the remaining sauce. If the pasta seems too dry, add 2–3 tbsp of the reserved water. Remember that fresh pasta absorbs a lot of liquid while it is sitting in the bowl. Serve at once with the optional cheese.

PASTA WITH MEAT & FISH SAUCES

Bucatini all'Amatriciana

BUCATINI WITH SMOKED PANCETTA AND TOMATO SAUCE

Serves 6 as a first course
or 4 as a main course

350g smoked pancetta cubes
1 tbsp olive oil
1 small onion, very finely
 chopped
sea salt and freshly ground
 black pepper
1 garlic clove, finely chopped
1 dried chilli, seeded and
 finely chopped
120ml dry white wine
450ml tomato sauce
 (version 2, page 96)
450g bucatini
6 tbsp freshly grated aged
 pecorino
freshly grated Parmesan,
 to serve

1 Put the pancetta and the oil in a non-stick frying pan and sauté until the fat has run out of the pancetta and the pancetta is crisp and browned. Stir frequently.

2 Add the onion and a pinch of salt to the frying pan and sauté for about 10 minutes. Mix in the garlic and chilli. Cook for a further minute or so and then splash in the wine. Turn the heat up and let the wine bubble away to reduce it by half. Pour in the tomato sauce and simmer for 15 minutes to allow the flavours to combine. Add salt and add pepper to your liking.

3 Cook the bucatini in plenty of boiling salted water until al dente. Drain thoroughly, giving the colander a few sharp shakes so that the water trapped in the bucatini comes out. Transfer the pasta to a heated bowl and mix in three-quarters of the sauce and the pecorino. Toss very thoroughly and then spoon the rest of the sauce over the top. Serve immediately, handing round the Parmesan separately in a bowl.

Amatrice is a town on the central Apennines where on 15 August huge cauldrons of this dish are prepared for the local *festa*. The sauce is traditionally made with pork jowl, and flavoured with a lot of dried chilli and grated pecorino to counterbalance the fattiness of the meat. In Britain I use pancetta – usually smoked – sold in cubes.

Tagliatelle al Ragù
TAGLIATELLE WITH BOLOGNESE SAUCE

Serves 6 as a first course
or 4 as a main course

For the bolognese sauce
30g unsalted butter
3 tbsp extra virgin olive oil
60g unsmoked pancetta or
 streaky bacon, finely chopped
1 small onion, finely chopped
½ carrot, finely chopped
1 celery stick, finely chopped
1 garlic clove, finely chopped
1 bay leaf
350g lean chuck or braising
 beef, minced
1 tbsp tomato purée
150ml red wine
150ml chicken stock
2 pinches grated nutmeg
sea salt and freshly ground
 black pepper
home-made tagliatelle, made
 with 3 large eggs and
 300g Italian 00 flour
 (page 85), or 450g Italian
 dried egg tagliatelle
freshly grated Parmesan,
 to serve

The early emigrants from southern Italy to the US took their beloved spaghetti with them. In America, when they opened their restaurants, they realised that the locals were great meat lovers. Thus, instead of introducing spaghetti with the traditional tomato sauce, the Italians had the clever idea – financially clever, but not gastronomically – of serving spaghetti with a meat sauce or meat balls. The meat sauce was a watered-down version, both literally and figuratively, of the *ragù bolognese*. It quickly caught on, and spaghetti bolognese became synonymous with Italian cooking. But in fact there is no combination of pasta and sauce that is less typically Italian!

In Bologna, *ragù* is used to dress the local pasta – tagliatelle, not spaghetti – fresh, home-made with eggs and local soft-wheat flour. And what a wonderful dish it is. If you cannot afford the time to make your own tagliatelle, remember that dried egg tagliatelle made by a reputable Italian producer are often better than fresh shop-bought pasta made with inferior flour, a minimum of eggs and a lot of water.

1 To make the bolognese sauce, heat the butter and oil in a heavy saucepan and cook the pancetta for 2 minutes, stirring constantly.

2 Add the onion, and when it has begun to soften add the carrot, celery, garlic and bay leaf. Cook for a further 10 minutes, stirring frequently.

3 Put in the minced beef and cook to brown it as much as possible, crumbling it in the pan with a fork. Do this over a high heat so that the meat browns rather than stews.

4 Add the tomato purée and continue to cook over a high heat for a further 2 minutes. Still over a high heat, splash in the wine and boil to evaporate. Remove and discard the bay leaf and pour in the stock. Season with the nutmeg, salt and pepper. Mix well and simmer, uncovered, for about 2 hours. Stir occasionally and add a little hot water if the sauce is too dry. The *ragù* should cook very slowly indeed, at the lowest possible simmer.

5 Cook the pasta in plenty of boiling salted water. Fresh pasta cooks quickly, so stay around and test after 1½ minutes. Drain as soon as it is al dente, reserving a cupful of the pasta water.

6 Return half the pasta to the hot saucepan and stir in about half the *ragù*. Pour in the rest of the tagliatelle and the rest of the *ragù*. Mix very well, adding 2–3 tbsp of the reserved water if the pasta seems dry. Transfer to a heated bowl or deep dish and serve immediately, handing the cheese round separately.

Tagliolini Verdi col Salmone e i Funghi

GREEN TAGLIOLINI WITH A SALMON AND MUSHROOM SAUCE

Serves 3–4

20g dried porcini
350g piece of fresh salmon
250ml fish or vegetable stock
120ml dry white wine
75g unsalted butter
1 shallot, very finely chopped
sea salt and freshly ground
 black pepper
180g cultivated fresh
 mushrooms, cleaned and
 coarsely chopped
1½ tbsp flour
3 tbsp double cream
home-made green tagliolini,
 made with 2 large eggs,
 225g Italian 00 flour and
 150g cooked or frozen spinach
 (page 89), or 350g dried
 green tagliolini or tagliatelle
bunch of fresh dill, chopped
freshly grated Parmesan,
 to serve

In no way can I claim this to be a traditional Italian dish. It is an Anna Del Conte invention, good enough to pass on. It is definitely a *piatto unico* (one-course meal), with a good salad to be served afterwards, but not with it. If you cannot find green dried egg pasta, use the usual common yellow variety.

1   Put the dried porcini in a small bowl and cover with very hot water. Set aside to soak for about 30 minutes.

2   Meanwhile, put the salmon in a saucepan and cover with the stock and wine. Bring to the boil and boil for 1 minute. Remove from the heat and leave the salmon in the pan to finish cooking while you prepare the sauce.

3   Put half the butter and the shallot in a heavy saucepan. Sprinkle with a little salt and cook gently until the shallot is soft, stirring occasionally.

4   Lift the porcini out of the soaking water. If they are very dirty, rinse them under cold water. Dry and chop them coarsely. Filter the porcini liquid through a sieve lined with muslin to catch any grit, and reserve.

5   Add the chopped porcini to the shallot and sauté gently for 5 minutes. Mix in the cultivated mushrooms, turn the heat up and cook until the liquid has come out of the mushrooms. Stir frequently.

6   Lift the fish out of the stock and place it on a board. Strain the stock and reserve.

7   Blend the flour into the mushroom sauce and cook for a minute or so, stirring constantly. Pour over a cupful of the fish stock and stir rapidly over a very low heat until smoothly blended. Add the rest of the stock very gradually, stirring constantly. Add 2–3 tbsp of the filtered porcini liquid. The sauce should be quite thin.

8 Bring the sauce slowly to the boil, then turn the heat right down, so that only a few bubbles break the surface of the sauce every now and then, and cook for 30 minutes. I use a flame diffuser. Alternatively you can cook the sauce in a bain-marie: place the pan containing the sauce in another saucepan of gently simmering water. You can of course simmer your mushroom sauce for only 5 minutes, but you will not achieve the same velvety, delicate yet rich sauce. At the end mix in the cream. Taste and adjust the seasoning.

9 Skin and bone the fish and flake the flesh. Add to the sauce and keep warm.

10 Cook the tagliolini in plenty of boiling salted water until al dente. Drain and return them to the hot saucepan in which they cooked. Toss with the remaining butter. Transfer to a heated bowl and cover with the sauce. Sprinkle the dill over the top just before serving. Pass the grated Parmesan round in a bowl.

Tonnarelli alla Pure di Tonno
TONNARELLI WITH TUNA AND ANCHOVY PURÉE

Serves 4 as a first course
or 3 as a main course

200g Italian or Spanish
 canned tuna packed in olive
 oil, drained
1½ salted anchovies, boned
 and rinsed, or 3 canned
 anchovy fillets
3 tbsp pine nuts
3 tbsp freshly grated
 Parmesan
sea salt and freshly ground
 black pepper
4 tbsp extra virgin olive oil
home-made tonnarelli,
 made with 2 large eggs
 and 200g Italian 00 flour
 (page 85), or 350g Italian
 dried egg tonnarelli or dried
 egg spaghetti

1 Put the tuna, anchovies, pine nuts, cheese and pepper to taste in a food processor. Process while gradually adding the olive oil.
2 Slide the pasta into a saucepan of boiling water, to which only 1 tbsp salt has been added. (The sauce is quite salty.) Cook until al dente.
3 Scoop out a cupful of the pasta water and add about 6 tbsp of it to the sauce through the funnel of the processor. The sauce should have the consistency of a thin béchamel. Taste and check the pepper.
4 Drain the tonnarelli and turn it into a heated bowl. Pour the sauce over it and toss thoroughly. Serve immediately.

In most supermarkets the canned tuna on sale is skipjack, an inferior variety of the tunny fish family, smaller in size, coarser in taste and less flavourful than the Mediterranean tunny. I strongly advise you to buy the better-quality tunny produced in France, Spain or Italy and preserved in olive oil. It is more expensive, but it is a very superior product. And it is absolutely necessary for this delicate creamy sauce.
Tonnarelli are a kind of square home-made pasta, particularly suitable for a smooth fish sauce.

Pasta con le Sarde
PASTA WITH FRESH SARDINES

Serves 4 as a main course

50g currants
6 tbsp extra virgin olive oil
1 red or Spanish onion, very
  finely sliced
sea salt and freshly ground
  black pepper
4 tbsp pine nuts
200g wild or cultivated fennel
  leaves
2 salted anchovies, boned and
  rinsed, or 4 canned anchovy
  fillets
450g fresh sardines, boned
  (see Note)
1 tsp fennel seeds
350g bucatini

*The dish can be prepared a
few hours in advance and then
baked for an extra 15 minutes
to heat the pasta through.*

This dish from Sicily is like a history of the island on a plate: part Greek, part Saracen, part Norman. The sardines and the wild fennel, typical food of the ancient Greeks, are here used to dress the most Italian of all foods, pasta. The dressing is lightened and made more interesting by the inclusion of pine nuts and currants, a Saracen influence, and the finished dish is cooked in the oven, a method brought to the island by the Normans. If you cannot get hold of wild or cultivated fennel leaves, use a small fennel bulb, cut into strips, together with its feathery green top.

1 Soak the currants in warm water for 10 minutes. Drain and dry well with kitchen paper.
2 Put 2 tbsp of the oil in a frying pan, add the onion and a pinch of salt, and sauté gently for 15 minutes, stirring frequently, until soft. Mix in the currants and the pine nuts and cook for a further 2 minutes.
3 Meanwhile, blanch the fennel leaves in a large saucepan of boiling salted water for 1 minute. (If you are using fennel bulb, cook until soft.) Lift the fennel out of the water with a slotted spoon, drain and dry with kitchen paper. Reserve the water in which it has cooked. Chop the fennel and add to the onion mixture. Cook over a very low heat for 10–15 minutes, adding 2–3 tbsp of the fennel water whenever the mixture appears too dry.
4 Heat the oven to 200°C/Gas Mark 6.
5 Chop about half the sardines and the anchovies and add to the pan with the fennel seeds and a generous grinding of pepper. Cook gently for 10 minutes, stirring frequently and adding more fennel water whenever necessary. Taste and adjust the seasoning.

Recipe continued overleaf

PASTA WITH FRESH SARDINES

continued

6 Heat 2 tbsp of the remaining oil in a non-stick frying pan. When the oil is very hot, but not yet smoking, slide in the remaining whole sardines and fry on both sides for 5 minutes.

7 Meanwhile, cook the pasta in the fennel water until very al dente. Drain, return the pasta to the pan and dress immediately with the sardine sauce.

8 Grease an oven dish with a little oil and transfer the pasta to it. Lay the fried sardines over the pasta, dribble with the rest of the oil and cover with foil. Bake for 15 minutes.

Note: To clean and bone fresh sardines, snap off the head of each fish and pull it away, thus removing most of the inside. Remove the back fin by pulling it off, starting from the tail end. Hold the sardine with one hand and open the belly with the thumb of the other hand, running it against the spine on both sides.

Open the fish, butterfly-fashion, and pull the spine sharply from the head end towards the tail end, giving a last sharp tug to remove the tail. Wash and dry the boned fish.

Spaghetti alla Carbonara
SPAGHETTI WITH EGGS AND BACON

Serves 4 as a first course
or 3 as a main course

1 tbsp olive oil
4 fresh sage leaves
1 garlic clove, peeled
120g smoked pancetta or
  smoked streaky bacon,
  cut into matchsticks
350g spaghetti
3 large eggs
6 tbsp freshly grated
  Parmesan
sea salt and freshly ground
  black pepper
60g unsalted butter

1   Heat the oil, sage leaves and garlic clove in a large frying pan. Add the pancetta and sauté for about 10 minutes, until the pancetta is golden brown and the fat has run out. Discard the garlic and the sage.
2   Cook the spaghetti in plenty of boiling salted water until al dente.
3   Meanwhile, lightly beat the eggs in a bowl and add the Parmesan, a little salt and a generous amount of black pepper.
4   Drain the pasta, reserving a cupful of the water. Return the spaghetti to the saucepan and toss with the butter, then add to the frying pan. Stir-fry for a minute or so.
5   Remove from the heat and transfer the spaghetti mixture to a heated bowl. Pour the egg and cheese mixture over the spaghetti, turn off the heat and stir thoroughly with 2 forks before you bring the frying pan straight to the table.

The creation of this dish is attributed to the *carbonari* – charcoal burners – who used to make their charcoal in the mountainous forests of Lazio. Traditionally, the meat used was the jowl of the pig, but nowadays most carbonara is made with pancetta, which is belly of pork, similar to streaky bacon but differently cured.

Pappardelle con la Lepre
PAPPARDELLE WITH HARE

Serves 5–6 as a main course

2 tbsp olive oil
75g unsalted butter
30g unsmoked pancetta,
 chopped
1 small onion, very finely
 chopped
1 small celery stick, very
 finely chopped
1 garlic clove, finely chopped
small sprig of rosemary,
 finely chopped
the legs of 1 hare
150ml red wine
2 level tsp plain flour
 or Italian 00 flour
150ml chicken stock
sea salt and freshly ground
 black pepper
pinch of grated nutmeg
2 tbsp double cream
home-made pappardelle,
 made with 3 large eggs and
 300g Italian 00 flour
 (page 85), or 450g Italian
 dried egg pappardelle or
 tagliatelle

1   Heat the oil and half the butter in a sauté pan and cook the pancetta for 2 minutes, stirring constantly. Add the onion and sauté for a further 5 minutes, stirring very frequently. Add the celery, garlic and rosemary and cook until soft. Push the *soffritto* to one side of the pan.

2   Add the hare legs and brown well on all sides. Raise the heat, pour over the wine and boil until the liquid has reduced by half.

3   Transfer the hare to a plate. Stir the flour into the cooking juices. Cook for 1 minute and then pour in half the stock. Mix well. Return the hare to the pan and season with salt and nutmeg. Turn the heat down to very low and cook gently for a good hour, and the lid slightly askew. If the sauce gets too dry add a little of the remaining stock. The sauce should in the end be rather thick.

4   Remove the hare from the pan. Bone the legs and cut the meat into very small pieces. Return the meat to the pan and add the cream and pepper to taste. Cook for about 2 minutes, stirring constantly. Taste and adjust the seasoning, then remove from the heat. Reheat the sauce before adding to the pasta.

5   Cook the pasta in plenty of boiling salted water until al dente, remembering that if you are using fresh home-made pasta it will only take about 1 minute to cook. Drain and turn the pasta into a heated bowl. Add the remaining butter and spoon over the hot hare sauce. Serve at once.

Only the legs of the hare are used for this dish. You can roast the saddle as they do in Tuscany, which is where this dish originally comes from. It is a rich dish, and is regarded as a *piatto unico* – one-course meal – even in Italy, where pasta is usually only the first course.

BAKED AND STUFFED PASTA

Ravioli con Carne
MEAT RAVIOLI

Serves 4 as a main course

For the pasta dough
300g Italian 00 flour
3 eggs

For the filling
1 tbsp olive oil
75g unsmoked pancetta,
 very finely chopped
350g lean minced beef
150ml meat stock
1 sprig of rosemary
sea salt and freshly ground
 black pepper
100g Parmesan, freshly grated
1 egg
¼ tsp ground cinnamon

For the dressing
60g unsalted butter
2 bruised garlic cloves
6–8 fresh sage leaves, torn
 into smallish pieces
75g Parmesan, freshly grated

When I was a child in Milan, ravioli were one of the dishes I loved to make. They can be filled with meat, pumpkin, spinach or even fish. Meat ravioli were my favourite and, indeed, are the traditional – and the most popular – ravioli, served with melted butter flavoured with fresh sage and garlic. Here is my family recipe.

Recipe continued overleaf

MEAT RAVIOLI
continued

1   First make the pasta dough (page 85) and leave it wrapped in cling film while you make the filling.

2   To prepare the filling: heat the oil and pancetta in a saucepan and, after about 5 minutes, throw in the minced beef. Fry the meat, breaking it up with a fork so that it all gets properly browned, which will take just over 5 minutes. Pour in the stock, then add the sprig of rosemary and the salt and pepper, and cook gently for about 30 minutes. Stir frequently.

3   When the meat is cooked, discard the rosemary sprig, spoon the mince into a bowl and let it cool for 10–15 minutes. Mix in 50g of the cheese, together with the egg and the cinnamon. Taste and check the seasoning.

4   Now start kneading the pasta dough, by hand or by machine, and when this is done make the ravioli.

5   Put the pasta dough on the work surface and cut off about one-quarter, leaving the rest wrapped in cling film. Thin the dough down in the pasta machine notch by notch as far as the last but one notch, as described on page 87. If you are rolling out by hand, roll the dough out as thin as you possibly can.

6   Work on one strip of dough at a time, keeping the remaining strips covered with a clean tea towel. Place mounds of the filling (about ½ tsp each) in a straight line along the length of the strip of dough, spacing them about 4cm apart and the same distance from the one long edge. Fold the dough lengthways over the filling and, using a pastry wheel, trim the edges where they meet. Then cut into squares between each mound of filling. Separate the squares and squeeze out any air that may be caught in the ravioli. Seal them tight with moistened fingers.

7   Place the ravioli, well separated, on clean dry tea towels. Cut off another quarter of the dough, knead in any trimmings from the previous batch and thin the strip down as before. If you are rolling out by hand, keep the dough you are not working on well covered or it will dry up and become brittle. Continue making more ravioli until you have used up all the filling and/or all the dough. Leave the ravioli uncovered until they are properly dry; you can then cover them with another cloth.

8 Bring a large saucepan of water to the boil with 1½ tbsp salt. Drop the ravioli gently into the pan. (If your saucepan is not large enough, cook the ravioli in 2 batches and keep the first batch warm in a very low oven, dressed with some of the flavoured butter – see step 9.) Give the ravioli a gentle stir with a wooden spoon and cook in simmering water – not fast-boiling or the ravioli might break – for 3–4 minutes until they are done. The best way to tell if they are done is to try one: the pasta should be still firm to the bite – al dente – round the edge. Lift the ravioli out with a slotted spoon and transfer them immediately to a heated and buttered bowl. Pat them dry with kitchen paper.

9 While the ravioli are cooking, make the dressing. Melt the butter in a small saucepan with the bruised garlic and the sage leaves. Fry gently until the sage leaves start to sizzle and the butter begins to turn golden. Remove and discard the garlic. Pour this simple dressing over the ravioli as soon as they are cooked and sprinkle with Parmesan. Serve at once, handing round the remaining cheese in a separate bowl.

Lasagne al Forno
BAKED LASAGNE

Serves 4–6

home-made lasagne made with
 3 large eggs and 300g Italian
 00 flour (page 85), or
 500g Italian dried egg lasagne
bolognese sauce (page 102)
1 tbsp sea salt
1 tbsp vegetable or olive oil
75g Parmesan, freshly grated
15g unsalted butter

For the béchamel sauce
750ml full-fat milk
75g unsalted butter
60g flour flavoured with
 2 pinches of grated nutmeg

1 If you are making your own lasagne, lay the pasta rectangles out, separate from each other, on clean tea towels.

2 While the bolognese sauce is cooking, make the béchamel. You will find the recipe on page 138.

3 Choose a large sauté pan. Fill it with water and add the salt and oil. When the water is boiling, slide in 5 or 6 lasagne at a time. Move them around with a wooden fork to stop them sticking to each other. When they are al dente, lift them out with a fish slice and plunge them into a bowl of cold water. Lift out, lay on cloths and pat dry with kitchen paper.

4 Heat the oven to 220°C/Gas Mark 7.

5 Butter a 30 x 20cm ovenproof dish. Spread 2 tbsp of the bolognese sauce on the bottom. Cover with a layer of lasagne and spread 2 tbsp or so of bolognese over the pasta, followed by the same of béchamel sauce. Sprinkle with a little Parmesan. Repeat, building up the dish in thin layers until you have used up all the ingredients. The top layer must be béchamel.

6 Dot with the butter and bake for 20 minutes. Remove from the oven and allow to rest for at least 5 minutes before serving so the flavours have time to develop.

Few dishes have been so badly copied abroad as baked lasagne, a dish that surely has acquired an appalling image. Yet when well made it is one of the finest creations of the very rich Bolognese cuisine.
This is a party dish, perfect for a family celebration.

Il Raviolone
PASTA AND SPINACH ROLL

Serves 8 as a first course
or 6 as a main course

700g frozen leaf spinach,
    thawed, or 1.25kg fresh
    spinach
sea salt and freshly ground
    black pepper
3 tbsp very finely chopped
    shallots
30g unsalted butter
225g fresh ricotta
90g Parmesan, freshly grated
½ tsp grated nutmeg
1 egg yolk
home-made pasta dough,
    made with 200g Italian 00
    flour, the yolks of 4 large
    eggs and just enough cold
    water to help the dough
    absorb the flour (page 85)
4 large slices of unsmoked
    ham

For dressing the roll
90g unsalted butter, heated
    with 1 bruised garlic clove
    and 4–6 fresh sage leaves,
    or a thin béchamel sauce
    (see Note opposite)
freshly grated Parmesan

In this dish the procedure for stuffing pasta is different. The whole sheet of pasta dough is rolled around the spinach filling. The roll is sliced when cold, just like a meat joint, and then heated up in the oven with its sauce. It results in a very attractive presentation.

1   If you are using frozen spinach, cook the thawed spinach in a covered pan with a little salt for 5 minutes. If you are using fresh spinach, discard any wilted or discoloured spinach leaves and the tougher stalks. Wash it, and then cook in a covered pan with just the water that clings to the leaves and with a little salt for 5–8 minutes, or until tender. Drain the spinach, squeezing lightly to remove most of its moisture. Set aside.

2   In a frying pan, sauté the chopped shallot in the butter over a moderate heat. When the shallot turns pale gold in colour, add the spinach and sauté for 5 minutes, turning the spinach over and over to *insaporire* – take up the flavour.

3   Transfer the contents of the frying pan to a food processor and add the ricotta, grated Parmesan, nutmeg, and, last of all, the egg yolk. Process for a few seconds. Check the seasoning.

4   Roll out the pasta dough into as thin a sheet as possible, about 50 x 35–40cm. Lay it flat in front of you. Square the sides to make a neat rectangle.

5   Place the ham slices to cover the pasta rectangle completely, leaving a clean edge of about 2.5m on all sides.

6   Spread the spinach filling over the ham. Roll up as for a Swiss roll by first making a pleat and then rolling fairly tightly. Wrap the pasta roll tightly in muslin and tie the two ends securely with string.

7   Use a fish kettle or other long, deep pan that can hold the roll comfortably and about 4 litres of water. Bring the water to the boil, add about 2 tbsp of salt and then put in the pasta roll. Cook at a gentle but steady boil for 35 minutes.

8 Lift out the roll. Unwrap it while it is hot and set it aside to cool, when it will be easier to carve.

9 Heat the oven to 200°C/Gas Mark 6.

10 Cut the roll into 1cm slices with a very sharp knife or an electric knife. (It is easier to slice the *rotolo* when cool.)

11 Place the slices in a generously buttered shallow baking dish, overlapping them a little. You can dress the slices with either the garlic- and sage-flavoured butter and then a generous amount of Parmesan, or with a layer of Parmesan covered with the thin, well-flavoured béchamel. Cover the dish with foil and bake for 15–20 minutes. Remove from the oven and leave for 5 minutes before serving.

Note: For a thin béchamel, use 750ml full-fat milk, 75g unsalted butter and 45g flour. Follow the recipe on page 138, heating the milk with 1 bay leaf.

Pasta 'Ncaciata
AUBERGINE AND RIGATONI CAKE

Serves 4–5 as a main course

2 aubergines, total weight
 about 450g
sea salt and freshly ground
 black pepper
vegetable oil for frying
450g penne or rigatoni
60g unsalted butter
double quantity tomato sauce
 (version 2, page 96)
225g Italian mozzarella cheese,
 coarsely grated or chopped
4 tbsp freshly grated Parmesan
4 tbsp freshly grated aged
 pecorino
1 level tbsp dried oregano
2 tbsp dried white breadcrumbs

1   Cut the aubergines into 6mm slices. Place a board on the slant over the sink. Put layers of aubergine slices on the board, sprinkling each layer with salt. Leave to drain for 1 hour. Rinse thoroughly and pat each slice dry.

2   Heat enough oil in a large frying pan to come about 2.5cm up the sides of the pan. The oil is hot enough when a corner of an aubergine slice dipped into it sizzles. Slide in a few slices of aubergine at a time and fry until deep golden on both sides. Do not overcrowd the slices or they will not fry properly.

3   Remove the fried aubergines with a slotted spoon, drain well and place in a dish lined with kitchen paper.

4   Cook the rigatoni in plenty of boiling salted water until very al dente. Drain and return the rigatoni to the saucepan in which they were cooked and toss with the butter. Mix in the tomato sauce, the three cheeses, oregano and pepper to taste. Check the seasoning.

5   Heat the oven to 190°C/Gas Mark 5.

6   Line the bottom of a 20cm springform cake tin with aubergine slices. Fill in any gaps with cut-up pieces of aubergine. Line the sides of the tin with aubergine slices, cutting to fit. Place any aubergine left over on the bottom of the tin. Fill the tin with the rigatoni mixture and press down lightly. Sprinkle with the breadcrumbs.

7   Bake for 20 minutes or until the filling is hot.

8   Remove from the oven and run a palette knife around the side of the tin. Place a heated round serving dish over the top of the tin and turn the tin upside down. Tap the base of the tin and give the dish a sharp shake or two. Unclip the ring and lift the tin away carefully. If necessary, press into place any pieces of aubergine stuck to the tin. Allow the cake to stand for at least 5 minutes for the flavours to combine.

This is a very showy southern Italian dish traditionally baked in a dome-shaped container, which can be tricky to unmould. In this recipe I suggest using a springform tin. It can be prepared a few hours in advance.

Pasta al Gratin
MACARONI CHEESE

Serves 4 as a first course
or 3 as a main course

60g fontina, grated
60g Parmesan, freshly grated
350g penne or macaroni

For the béchamel sauce
750ml full-fat milk
75g unsalted butter
60g flour, preferably
 Italian 00 flour
sea salt and freshly ground
 black pepper
grated nutmeg

Years ago, at the beginning of my married life in England, my husband asked me which was my favourite pasta dish. 'Very difficult question,' I answered. Recently, however, when he asked me the same question, I said, 'Pasta al gratin.' 'Oh really?' he said, and thought, 'What about that discerning palate she's so proud of?' But he was thinking of the macaroni cheese of his schooldays, and I was thinking of the velvety, cheesy delight of Pasta al Gratin.

Although it is made with a sauce with a French name, the dish is Italian. It is made in many regions, with certain variations. In the north, for instance, Parmesan is used, sometimes mixed with Emmental or with fontina, as in my recipe, while in Naples a buffalo mozzarella is cut up and pushed here and there among the penne.

For all its simplicity, Pasta al Gratin needs a careful and patient cook, able to make a velvety béchamel and to drain the pasta at the right time, i.e. when still slightly undercooked, so that it can reach the right texture during baking.

Recipe continued overleaf

MACARONI CHEESE

continued

1   To make the béchamel sauce, heat the milk until hot but not boiling. Draw off the heat.

2   Melt the butter, draw the saucepan off the heat and stir in the flour. Put the pan back on the heat and cook, stirring constantly, for about 30 seconds.

3   Draw the pan off the heat and add the milk gradually. At the beginning add only a couple of tablespoons and incorporate well, before adding another few tablespoons. Adding the milk slowly in this way helps prevent the flour forming lumps. Return the pan to the heat and cook until the sauce comes to the boil. Season with salt and pepper and with a generous grating of nutmeg. Cook for a few minutes, stirring constantly.

4   To finish the sauce you can either use a flame diffuser under the pan or a bain-marie. Leave the sauce to cook very, very gently for 10–15 minutes; you only need to stir occasionally. This long slow cooking makes a rich velvety sauce that you would not be able to achieve if you only cooked the béchamel for a shorter time, that is, just enough to cook the flour.

5   Add the cheeses to the béchamel. Taste and adjust the seasoning.

6   Cook the pasta in plenty of boiling salted water until very al dente. Drain thoroughly (penne tend to hold water in their hollows).

7   Heat the oven to 180°C/Gas Mark 4.

8   Coat a shallow baking dish (about 5cm deep) with a little of the sauce. Dress the pasta with about two-thirds of the béchamel and transfer to the prepared dish. Spread the rest of the sauce all over the top. Bake for about 30 minutes, until the penne at the top begin to brown.

9   Leave out of the oven for 5 minutes before serving, to allow the flavours to blend while cooling a little.

OTHER FAVOURITES

Tagliatelle al Burro e Formaggio
TAGLIATELLE WITH BUTTER AND PARMESAN

Serves 4 as a first course
or 3 as a main course

home-made tagliatelle, made
  with 2 large eggs and
  200g Italian 00 flour
  (page 85), or 400g Italian
  dried egg tagliatelle
sea salt
60g Parmesan, freshly grated,
  plus extra for serving
60g best-quality unsalted
  butter

1 Cook the pasta in plenty of boiling salted water until al dente. Drain – but do not overdrain – and turn half the pasta into a heated serving bowl. Add about 4 tbsp of the cheese and stir well.

2 Cut the butter into small pieces and add half to the bowl. Toss thoroughly, then add the remaining cheese. Add the remaining butter and toss until all the butter has melted. Serve at once and top with more grated cheese.

In my home in Milan when I was a child, special butter was used for this sauce. The best farm butter was sold, cut in pieces and wrapped in muslin, by the best delicatessen in Via Monte Napoleone. And the tagliatelle were, of course, home-made.

This recipe is characteristic of northern Italian cooking. It is also the dressing used when you are lucky enough to have a white truffle to shave over it. To do the dish justice, you should make your own pasta and buy the best unsalted butter, as well as making sure your Parmesan is a proper Parmigiano-Reggiano, of which you grate an ample quantity just before serving.

Tagliolini Piccanti Freddi
TAGLIOLINI WITH A PIQUANT SUN-DRIED TOMATO SAUCE

Serves 4 as a first course

300g sun-dried tomatoes
 in olive oil
6 tbsp extra virgin olive oil
1 or 2 dried chillies, according
 to taste, strength and size,
 seeded and crumbled
5 garlic cloves, bruised
12 fresh basil leaves, torn into
 small pieces
home-made tagliolini made
 with 2 large eggs and
 200g Italian 00 flour
 (page 85), or 300g Italian
 dried egg tagliolini or
 spaghetti
sea salt
75g plain black olives, such as
 Kalamata

1   Cut the sundried tomatoes in thin strips and put them in a bowl large enough to hold the pasta later. Add the oil, chillies, garlic and basil.
2   Cook the tagliolini in plenty of boiling salted water. Drain it when it is even more al dente than you would like for eating it hot. (Overcooked cold pasta is really unpleasant.) Turn the pasta into the bowl and toss very thoroughly, lifting the strands up high so as to separate them. Leave to infuse for 2 hours or so, then fish out the garlic and discard. Scatter with the olives and serve.

I do not usually like cold pasta, but I make a few exceptions.
This is the best cold pasta dish I know, and it has always been a great success at my demonstrations. When I have not got the time or the inclination to make my tagliolini, I prefer to buy the best brand (which usually means the most expensive) of Italian dried tagliolini or tagliatelle.

Farfalle e Zucchine al Sugo di Pistacchio e Basilico

FARFALLE AND COURGETTES WITH A PISTACHIO NUT AND BASIL SAUCE

Serves 6 as a first course
or 4 as a main course

200ml extra virgin olive oil,
  preferably from Sicily or
  Puglia
4 garlic cloves, bruised
600g courgettes, cut into
  matchsticks
sea salt and freshly ground
  black pepper
120g shelled pistachio nuts
50g fresh basil
30g fresh flat-leaf parsley
500g dried farfalle
15g unsalted butter

1   Heat 2 tbsp of the oil and the garlic in a non-stick frying pan. When the oil is hot, add the courgettes and fry at a lively heat until golden all over. Shake the pan very often. They are ready when they are tender, not still crunchy but not yet soft, and when the flavour has fully developed, about 15 minutes. Season with salt and pepper.

2   While the zucchini are frying, put the pistachios into a small saucepan. Cover with water, bring to a boil, and boil for 10 seconds. Skin the pistachios, taking them out of the hot water a few at a time for easier peeling. Dry them thoroughly and put in a food processor.

3   Rinse and dry the basil and parsley and add to the pistachios. Process while adding the rest of the oil through the funnel. Stop the machine, push the mixture down from the side of the bowl, and process again a few seconds. Add salt and pepper to taste. Scoop out the mixture into a serving bowl and place the bowl in a warm oven.

4   Cook the pasta in plenty of salted boiling water until al dente. Drain, reserving a cupful of the pasta water, and turn immediately into the heated bowl. Add the butter and toss very thoroughly, adding 3 or 4 tbsp of the reserved water to give the pasta the right fluidity.

5   Spoon the zucchini and their juices over the top of the pasta and serve at once.

I first had this dish many years ago at a dinner party in a friend's house overlooking Catania, in Sicily. It remains high on the list of my favourite pasta dishes and I think its presentation and the combination of flavours epitomise the very best of Sicilian cooking. If you cannot make your own green pasta, buy the best Italian brand of egg tagliatelle, preferably green.

Conchiglie di Radicchio Rosso col Ripieno di Pasta

RED RADICCHIO LEAVES FILLED WITH PASTA

Serves 4 as a first course

1 garlic clove
2 salted anchovies, boned and
  rinsed or 4 canned anchovy
  fillets, drained
1 green chilli, seeded and cut
  into thin matchsticks
4 tbsp extra virgin olive oil
sea salt
225g ditali or gnocchi
4 outside leaves from a large
  head of red radicchio
freshly ground black pepper
  (optional)

1 Chop the parsley, garlic and anchovies and put them in a large bowl together with the chilli matchsticks. Beat in the oil and add salt to taste.

2 Cook the pasta in plenty of boiling salted water, remembering that cold pasta needs to be more al dente than hot pasta. Drain, refresh under cold water and drain again thoroughly. Pat dry with kitchen paper. Turn the pasta into the bowl with the dressing and toss well. Leave to infuse for about 2 hours.

3 Wash and dry the radicchio leaves thoroughly and lay them on individual plates. Taste and add pepper, if liked. Fill the salad leaves with the pasta just before serving.

Years ago, I read this short clip in *The Times*, which I shall always remember.

> Laurette Bruson threw macaroni salad at Richard, her groom, during a tiff at their wedding reception in Tampa, Florida, and he responded by shooting her with a .22 pistol.

I am not particularly fond of cold pasta salads but I doubt I would go that far, and I certainly wouldn't if I were eating this pasta salad, which I find particularly good. I use a peppery oil for this dish, such as an extra virgin oil from Chianti or a fruity and herby oil from Sicily or Puglia.

Spaghettini con le Cappe Sante
SPAGHETTINI WITH SCALLOPS

Serves 3-4

350g spaghettini (thin
 spaghetti)
sea salt
8 scallops
100ml extra virgin olive oil
2 garlic cloves, very finely
 chopped
2 tbsp chopped flat-leaf parsley
½ tsp dried chilli flakes
50g dried white breadcrumbs
sea salt

1   Cook the spaghettini in a large saucepan of salted boiling water.
2   While the pasta is cooking, clean the scallops, wash and dry them. Then separate the white meat from the coral and cut into pieces of about 2cm.
3   Heat the oil in a large frying pan and add the garlic, parsley and chilli. Stir-fry for 1 minute and then throw in the breadcrumbs. Fry, stirring the whole time, for a further minute to get the crumbs nice and golden all over before you add the white part of the scallops. Fry for another 30 seconds, by which time the pasta should be ready.
4   Drain the spaghettini, add to the frying pan and mix the ingredients together. Fry the whole thing for 1 minute, then add the coral and give it a final stir-fry of 1 minute. Serve immediately straight from the frying pan.

A quick and easy recipe which needs only perfect timing. You want the pasta and the scallops sauce to be ready at the same time for combining in the final stir-fry. Do not add the scallops to the *soffritto* – frying mixture – until the pasta is almost done, because they will get tough if cooked for longer.

RISOTTI

AND MORE

Risotto is a relative newcomer to the Italian culinary scene, where most dishes can trace their origins back to the Renaissance, if not to Roman times. It was only during the nineteenth century that risotto became popular in the northern regions of Italy – Piedmont, Lombardy and Veneto – where the rice was cultivated, as indeed it still is.

A genuine risotto, for all its apparent simplicity, is a challenge to most cooks. Although there are certain rules to observe, the feel of making a good risotto can only be learnt with practice. The first essential is to use top-quality ingredients. Secondly, one must remember that risotto is prepared according to a well-defined method. It is not just a mixture of rice and other ingredients, and it is certainly not, as some people have believed, a dish that Italians make from an assortment of leftovers. Rice is often the only ingredient, apart from flavourings. When there are other ingredients they are almost always cooked with the rice, so as to allow the flavours to combine and fuse.

The rice must be medium-grain white rice, which absorbs the liquid in which it cooks and which swells up without breaking or becoming mushy. Only 2 types of rice are suitable for making risotto: superfino and fino. Arborio, which is widely available, is the most popular variety of superfino rice and is suitable for all risotti. It has large plump grains with a delicious nutty taste when cooked. Carnaroli, a new superfino variety, is produced in relatively small quantities. It keeps its firm consistency, while its starch dissolves deliciously during the cooking. Vialone Nano, a fino rice, has a shorter, stubbier grain containing starch of a kind that does not soften easily in the cooking. It is my favourite rice for vegetable risotti. Vialone Nano cooks more quickly than Arborio – 15 minutes as opposed to 20 minutes for Arborio. Both Carnaroli and Vialone Nano can be found in specialist Italian shops. In most of the recipes I have specified the best variety of rice to use, bearing in mind availability.

The choice of saucepan is crucial to the success of the dish. The pan must be wide, heavy-bottomed and large enough to contain the rice when it has finished cooking, by which time it will have increased its volume by nearly 3 times. Ideally it should also be round-bottomed, to prevent the rice from sticking in the corners.

The quality of the stock is also very important. It should be made with meat, chicken or vegetables or top-quality stock cubes or powder. Italian stock for risotto is never made with lamb or pork. Vegetable stock is particularly suitable for a vegetable or fish risotto; for the latter a light fish stock is also good. If you have not got any stock already prepared, use good-quality meat stock cubes; there are some on the market that do not contain monosodium glutamate. Good-quality Italian rice takes about 15–20 minutes to cook, according to the variety. At the end of the cooking the rice should be al dente – firm but tender without a chalky centre – and the risotto should have a creamy consistency.

You will find here recipes for 12 risotti, many with vegetables, others with fish and with meat. These last are more nourishing and are definitely main course dishes, while the lighter risotti with vegetables can be the start, *all'Italiana*, of any dinner party.

Risotto should be eaten as soon as it is done, but if you do not like to cook when your guests have already arrived, you can make a *timballo* instead, and accompany it with a suitable sauce if you wish. For this, keep the risotto slightly undercooked, being careful to add the stock very gradually at the end of the cooking or the rice will be too liquid when it is ready. Spread the risotto out on a large dish and leave it to cool. When it is cold, spoon it into a ring mould that has been generously buttered and sprinkled with dried breadcrumbs.

Set the mould in a bain-marie and bake in the oven heated to 220°C/Gas Mark 7 for about 20 minutes. Loosen the risotto all round the mould with a palette knife. Place a large round platter over it and turn the whole thing upside-down. Give the mould a few taps on the top, shake the platter and mould vigorously and lift the mould away. If some of the risotto sticks to the mould, remove it and patch the shape up neatly. Nobody will notice, especially if you place some basil or parsley over it.

Risotto al Limone
RISOTTO WITH LEMON

Serves 4 as a first course
or 3 as a main course

1.25 litres chicken
  or vegetable stock
60g unsalted butter
1 tbsp olive oil
2 shallots, very finely chopped
1 celery stick, very finely
  chopped
300g Italian rice,
  preferably Arborio
½ organic lemon
5 or 6 fresh sage leaves
leaves from small sprig
  of fresh rosemary
1 egg yolk
4 tbsp freshly grated
  Parmesan
4 tbsp double cream
sea salt and freshly ground
  black pepper

1   Bring the stock to a gentle simmer (keep it simmering all through the cooking of the rice).
2   Heat half the butter, the oil, shallots and celery in a heavy-bottomed saucepan and sauté until the *soffritto* – frying mixture – of shallot and celery is softened (about 7 minutes). Mix in the rice and continue to sauté, stirring, until the rice is well coated with the fats and is partly translucent.
3   Pour over about 150ml of the simmering stock. Stir very thoroughly and cook until the rice has absorbed nearly all of the stock, still stirring. Add another ladleful of simmering stock, and continue in this manner until the rice is ready. You may not need all the stock. Good-quality Italian rice for risotto takes 15–20 minutes to cook.
4   Meanwhile, thinly pare the zest from the lemon half and chop it with the herbs. Mix into the rice halfway through the cooking.
5   Squeeze the half lemon into a small bowl and combine it with the egg yolk, Parmesan, cream, a little salt and a very generous grinding of black pepper. Mix well with a fork.
6   When the rice is al dente, draw the pan off the heat and stir in the egg and cream mixture and the remaining butter. Cover the pan and leave to rest for 2 minutes or so. Then give the risotto an energetic stir, transfer to a heated dish or bowl and serve at once, with more grated Parmesan in a little bowl if you wish.

This recipe first appeared in my book, *Secrets from an Italian Kitchen*. Friends and reviewers alike have all said they found it one of the best risotti ever, which is why I feel no qualms about including it in this book.

Risotto alla Milanese
RISOTTO WITH SAFFRON

Serves 4–5 as a first course
or as an accompaniment

1.5 litres chicken or meat
   stock
1 small onion, very finely
   chopped
75g unsalted butter
350g Italian rice,
   preferably Carnaroli
180ml good red wine
½ tsp powdered saffron
   or saffron strands crushed
   to a powder
sea salt and freshly ground
   black pepper
75g Parmesan, freshly grated

1   Bring the stock to simmering point (keep it at a very low simmer all through the cooking of the rice).

2   Put the onion and 60g of the butter in a heavy-bottomed saucepan and sauté until soft and translucent. Add the rice and stir until well coated with fat. Sauté until the rice is partly translucent. Pour in the wine and boil for 1 minute, stirring constantly, and then pour in 150ml of the simmering stock. Cook until nearly all the stock has been absorbed and then add another ladleful of the simmering stock. Continue cooking and adding small quantities of stock, while keeping the risotto at a steady lively simmer all the time. If you finish the stock before the rice is properly cooked, add a little boiling water.

3   About halfway through the cooking (good rice takes about 15–20 minutes to cook), add the saffron dissolved in a little stock. When the rice is al dente, taste and adjust the seasoning.

4   Draw the pan off the heat and mix in the rest of the butter and 4 tbsp of the Parmesan. Put the lid on and leave for 1 minute or so. When the butter and the Parmesan have melted, give the risotto a vigorous stir and transfer to a heated dish. Serve immediately, with the rest of the cheese handed round separately.

Some Italians have queried the use of red wine instead of white in this recipe. My answer is that not only in my own family – Milanese for generations – but in some very authoritative cookbooks the suggested wine is red. Other recipes do not include any wine, but add some cream or milk at the end. The choice is yours.
As for the saffron, the strands are definitely more reliable than the powder, but they must be added earlier in the cooking so as to dissolve well, thus losing some flavour during the cooking.
This is the risotto traditionally served with Ossobuco and with Cotolette alla Milanese, breaded veal cutlets.

Risotto al Pomodoro
RISOTTO WITH TOMATOES

Serves 4 as a first course
or 3 as a main course

700g ripe tomatoes, peeled
7 tbsp extra virgin olive oil
3 or 4 garlic cloves,
 thickly sliced
good handful of fresh basil
 leaves, torn into pieces
1.25 litres vegetable stock
300g Italian rice,
 preferably Carnaroli
sea salt and freshly ground
 black pepper

1 Cut the peeled tomatoes in half. Squeeze out and discard some of the seeds. Chop the tomatoes coarsely and put them in a heavy-bottomed saucepan large enough to hold the rice later. Remember that the rice will be nearly three times its original volume by the end of the cooking.

2 Add 4 tbsp of the oil to the pan, then add the garlic and half the basil. Cook briskly for 1–2 minutes, stirring.

3 Meanwhile, bring the stock to a simmer (keep it simmering very gently all through the making of the risotto).

4 Add the rice to the pan with the tomatoes and cook for about 2 minutes, stirring constantly.

5 Pour over a ladleful of simmering stock and continue cooking, adding more stock little by little until the rice is al dente. If you want to serve the risotto cold, remove it from the heat when the rice is slightly underdone; it finishes cooking as it cools.

6 Add salt and pepper to taste and mix in the rest of the oil. Transfer to a serving dish and sprinkle the remaining basil leaves on the top. If you serve the risotto cold, fluff it up with a fork before bringing it to the table.

The match of risotto with tomatoes is a modern one, but it is so good that I am sure it will become a classic. This risotto does not contain any butter. It is very light and fresh, and it is very good, if not better, cold.

Risotto al Peperone
RISOTTO WITH PEPPERS

Serves 4 as a first course
or 3 as a main course

2 large peppers, preferably
 1 yellow and 1 red
about 4 tbsp extra virgin
 olive oil
25g unsalted butter
2 garlic cloves, sliced
4 tbsp chopped flat-leaf parsley
4 tomatoes, peeled, seeded
 and chopped
1.25 litres vegetable stock
300g Italian rice, preferably
 Arborio or Vialone Nano
4 pinches of chilli powder
sea salt and freshly ground
 black pepper
12 fresh basil leaves

1 Wash and dry the peppers. Cut them into quarters and remove and discard the seeds, cores and white ribs. Cut them into thin strips about 2cm long. Set aside.

2 In a heavy-bottomed saucepan heat the butter and 2 tbsp of the oil. Throw in the garlic and half the parsley and, when they begin to sizzle, add the strips of pepper and cook for 5 minutes. Mix in the chopped tomatoes and continue cooking for a further 5 minutes, stirring frequently.

3 Meanwhile, in a separate saucepan bring the stock to a simmer.

4 Add the rice to the *soffritto* – frying mixture – and cook, stirring the whole time, for a minute or two. Now begin to add the simmering stock gradually, a ladleful at a time. Wait to add each subsequent ladleful until the previous one has nearly all been absorbed.

5 When the rice is nearly done, season with the chilli powder and salt and pepper to taste. Draw the pan off the heat and stir in the remaining 2 tbsp of oil and the rest of the parsley. Transfer to a heated deep serving dish, sprinkle with the basil leaves and serve at once.

Risotto, the staple of northern Italy, used never to be made with olive oil, the cooking fat of the south. The advantage of butter is that, when melted, it penetrates into the grains of the rice, which is what you want to happen, while oil makes a film around them. But some modern risotti are now made with a mixture of butter and oil, especially when oil is the ideal dressing for the accompanying ingredient, peppers in this case.

This is my adaptation of a traditional risotto from Voghera, a town in south-west Lombardy that is famous for its peppers.

Risotto alla Paesana
RISOTTO WITH VEGETABLES

Serves 4 as a first course
or 3 as a main course

100g podded fresh peas
225g asparagus
100g courgette
225g ripe firm tomatoes,
 peeled, or Italian canned
 or plum tomatoes, drained
4 tbsp extra virgin olive oil
bunch of fresh flat-leaf parsley,
 chopped
1 garlic clove, chopped
sea salt and freshly ground
 black pepper
1.25 litres chicken or
 vegetable stock
30g unsalted butter
2 shallots, chopped
250g Italian rice, preferably
 Carnaroli or Arborio
5 tbsp dry white wine
45g Parmesan, freshly grated
12 fresh basil leaves, torn
 into pieces

1   Cook the fresh peas in lightly salted boiling water until just tender. Meanwhile, trim and wash the asparagus and cook them in boiling salted water until al dente. Drain and cut the tender part of the spears into small pieces. (Reserve the rest for a soup or a mousse.) Blanch the courgette for 2–3 minutes, then drain and cut into small cubes. Cut the tomatoes in half, squeeze out the seeds and then cut into short strips.

2   Put half the oil, the parsley and garlic in a sauté pan and sauté for 1 minute. Stir in all the vegetables, season lightly with salt and sauté over a low heat for 2 minutes for them to take the flavour of the soffritto – the fried mixture. Set aside.

3   Heat the stock in a saucepan until just simmering (keep it simmering all through the cooking of the rice).

4   Put the rest of the oil and half the butter in a heavy-bottomed saucepan. Add the shallots and sauté until tender. Add the rice and stir to coat with the fats, then cook for 2 minutes or until partly translucent. Splash with the wine and boil rapidly to evaporate, stirring constantly. Add a ladleful of simmering stock and let the rice absorb it while you stir constantly. Continue to add the stock gradually, stirring frequently, until the rice is al dente. (This will take about 15–20 minutes.)

5   Halfway through the cooking, stir in the vegetables with all their cooking juices. Season with pepper; taste to check the salt.

6   When the rice is done, draw the pan off the heat and add the rest of the butter, cut into small pieces, and the Parmesan. Place the lid tightly on the pan and allow to stand for a couple of minutes. Then stir vigorously and transfer to a heated dish. Garnish with the basil leaves and serve at once.

This lovely fresh risotto is best made in the spring, when the new peas and asparagus are in season. The vegetables can be varied: you can put in a little celery and carrot when there is no asparagus; French beans are suitable too. Try to match the flavours of the vegetables so as not to have a strident note.

Risotto al Finocchio
RISOTTO WITH FENNEL

Serves 4–5 as a first course
or 3–4 as a main course

2 fennel bulbs, about 600g
1 tbsp olive oil
60g unsalted butter
1 small onion, finely chopped
1 celery stick, finely chopped
1.25 litres vegetable stock
sea salt and freshly ground
 black pepper
300g Italian rice,
 preferably Vialone Nano
6 tbsp dry white wine
4 tbsp double cream
50g Parmesan, freshly grated

1 Cut off and discard the fennel stalks, but keep some of the feathery foliage. Remove any bruised outer leaves and cut the bulbs lengthways in half. Slice the halves very finely across. Wash thoroughly and drain.

2 Put the oil, half the butter, the onion and celery in a smallish sauté pan. Sauté until the vegetables are pale gold. Add the sliced fennel and stir it over and over to let it take up the flavour. Add about 4 tbsp of the stock and cover the pan. Cook, stirring occasionally, for about 20 minutes or until the fennel is very soft. Mash it with a fork to a purée over a high heat, so that the excess liquid evaporates. Add salt to taste.

3 Bring the remaining stock to a gentle simmer (keep it simmering all through the cooking of the rice).

4 Heat the remaining butter in a heavy-bottomed saucepan. When the butter foam begins to subside, mix in the rice and stir to coat the grains thoroughly. Sauté for a couple of minutes until the rice is partly translucent. Turn the heat up and add the wine. Let it bubble away, stirring the rice constantly.

5 Now begin to add the simmering stock a ladleful at a time. When nearly all of the first ladleful has been absorbed, add another, always stirring the rice. If you run out of stock before the rice is done, add some boiling water and continue the cooking.

6 Halfway through the cooking of the rice, stir in the mashed fennel with all the cooking juices.

7 When the rice is al dente, draw the pan from the heat and add the cream, Parmesan and a generous grinding of pepper. Mix everything well together. Transfer to a heated dish, scatter the snipped fennel foliage over the top and serve at once.

Vegetable risotto is one of the great strengths of Venetian cooking. Of all of them, this fennel risotto is my favourite, especially when I can get hold of fennel that is full of flavour and not 'the commercial variety grown in Italy for export which is beautiful but dumb' as the late Jane Grigson so aptly put it.

Risotto coi Peoci
RISOTTO WITH MUSSELS

Serves 4 as a first course
or 3 as a main course

1.8 kg mussels
300ml dry white wine
4 tbsp chopped flat-leaf
 parsley
6 tbsp olive oil
3 shallots, very finely chopped
sea salt and freshly ground
 black pepper
1 litre light fish or vegetable
 stock
1 celery stick, with the leaves
 if possible
1 garlic clove
½ dried chilli, crumbled
300g Italian rice, preferably
 Carnaroli or Arborio

1 First clean the mussels. Scrape off the barnacles, tug off the beard and scrub thoroughly with a stiff brush under running water. Throw away any mussel that remains open after you have tapped it on a hard surface.

2 Put the wine in a large sauté pan, add the mussels and cover the pan. Cook over a high heat until the mussels are open, which will only take 3–4 minutes. Shake the pan every now and then.

3 As soon as the mussels are open, remove the meat from the shells and discard the shells. Strain the cooking liquid through a sieve lined with muslin, pouring it slowly and gently so that the sand will be left at the bottom of the pan.

4 Set aside a dozen of the nicest mussels; chop the rest and put in a bowl. Mix in the parsley.

5 Pour the oil into a heavy-bottomed saucepan. Add the shallots and a pinch of salt and sauté until the shallot is soft and just beginning to colour.

6 In another saucepan, heat the stock to simmering point (keep it just simmering all through the cooking of the rice).

7 Meanwhile, chop the celery and garlic together. Add to the shallot with the chilli. Sauté for a further minute or so. Now add the rice and stir to coat with oil, then cook it for a couple of minutes until partly translucent. Pour over the mussel liquid and stir well. When the liquid has been absorbed add the simmering stock, one ladleful at a time. Stir constantly at first. When the rice is nearly cooked, mix in the chopped mussels, then continue cooking until al dente.

8 Season with salt, if necessary, and pepper. Transfer to a heated dish and garnish with the reserved whole mussels.

I have always found a risotto with mussels to be rather unsatisfactory, because you either have only risotto in your mouth, albeit fish tasting, or else a large mussel. So one day I came up with the idea of chopping up most of the mussels so that morsels of them could be enjoyed in each mouthful. This is the recipe I developed and it works very well.

Risotto con le Animelle
RISOTTO WITH SWEETBREADS

Serves 4 as a main course

450g lamb sweetbreads
½ organic lemon
sea salt and freshly ground
 black pepper
1.25 litres chicken stock
120g unsalted butter
2 shallots, finely chopped
about 8 fresh sage leaves,
 snipped
300g Italian rice,
 preferably Arborio
6 tbsp dry white wine
4 tbsp Marsala (Madeira
 or port can also be used)
75g Parmesan, freshly grated

1 Soak the sweetbreads in cold water for at least 1 hour. Rinse them and put them in a pan with the half lemon and 1 tsp of sea salt. Cover with fresh cold water and bring to the boil. Boil for 2 minutes. Drain well, plunge into cold water and drain again. Remove all fat and the white tubes, as well as the hard bits. Put the sweetbreads between 2 plates with a weight on top to squeeze out all excess liquid. Dry them and cut them into morsels.

2 Heat the stock to simmering (keep it simmering all through the cooking of the risotto).

3 Melt half the butter in a heavy-bottomed saucepan. Add the shallots, 4 of the sage leaves and a pinch of salt and cook until the shallots are soft and translucent.

4 Add the rice and stir to coat with butter, then sauté for 2–3 minutes until partly translucent. Pour in the wine and boil for a minute or two until it has evaporated, stirring constantly. Now begin to add simmering stock, little by little, in the usual way. Do not add too much at one time or the risotto will not cook properly. Keep the heat lively and constant.

5 Meanwhile, melt half the remaining butter in a sauté or frying pan. Add the rest of the sage leaves. When the sage begins to sizzle, slide in the sweetbreads and sauté for 2 minutes, turning them over to brown on all sides. Add the Marsala to the pan and let it bubble away on a slow heat. Cook for 7–8 minutes, stirring occasionally.

6 When the rice is nearly done, pour the sweetbreads and all the juices into the risotto pan. Stir thoroughly. Taste and adjust the seasoning, and finish cooking the risotto.

7 When the rice is al dente, draw the pan off the heat. Add the remaining butter and a couple of spoonfuls of the Parmesan. Cover the pan tightly and let the butter melt for a minute or so, then stir the risotto gently but thoroughly. Transfer to a heated dish and serve at once, handing round the rest of the Parmesan in a bowl.

In restaurants, sweetbreads are often accompanied by boiled rice. That rather boring presentation has, however, led me to devise this dish, where the winey-syrupy sweetbreads are combined with a classic *risotto in bianco*.

During the truffle season a small white truffle shaved over the top of the risotto makes the dish truly sensational.

Risotto con le Sogliole
RISOTTO WITH DOVER SOLE

Serves 4 as a main course

75g unsalted butter
2 tbsp very finely chopped
 shallot
sea salt and freshly ground
 black pepper
1.25 litre light fish stock
350g Italian rice,
 preferably Carnaroli
120ml dry white wine
2 tbsp chopped fresh dill
350g skinless Dover sole
 fillets
4 tbsp freshly grated
 Parmesan

1   Heat 60g of the butter and the shallot in a heavy-bottomed saucepan. Add a pinch of salt and sauté until the shallot is soft and translucent.
2   Meanwhile, heat the fish stock in another saucepan to simmering (keep it at the lowest simmer all through the cooking of the risotto).
3   Add the rice to the shallot and stir to coat with butter, then sauté for a minute or so until partly translucent. Splash with wine and let it bubble away, stirring constantly.
4   Add about 150ml of simmering stock, stir well and let the rice absorb the liquid. Continue adding stock little by little until the rice is nearly done, then mix in half of the dill and continue the cooking.
5   Meanwhile, heat the remaining butter in a non-stick frying pan. Cut the fish fillets in half, across. Slide them into the butter and sauté for 3 minutes. Turn them over and sauté for a further minute. Sprinkle with salt and pepper.
6   When the rice is al dente, mix in the Parmesan and the juices from the fish fillets. Turn into a heated dish. Place the fish fillets neatly over the top and sprinkle with the remaining dill. Serve immediately.

It might seem extravagant to use Dover sole in a humble dish such as a risotto, but I assure you that it is necessary. You only need a small amount of Dover sole, and it does make a great difference to the dish. The delicacy and firm texture of the fish is in perfect harmony with the soft creaminess of the risotto; none of the other ingredients disturbs this happy balance of flavours.

Risotto con la Salsiccia
RISOTTO WITH SAUSAGE

Serves 4 as a first course
or 3 as a main course

350g luganega sausage or
  other pure pork, coarse-
  grained, continental sausage
2 tbsp olive oil
1 sprig of fresh sage
150ml full-bodied red wine,
  such as Barbera
1.25 litres chicken stock
45g unsalted butter
2 or 3 shallots, depending
  on size, finely chopped
300g Italian rice, preferably
  Arborio or Carnaroli
sea salt and freshly ground
  black pepper
freshly grated Parmesan,
  to serve (optional)

1   Skin the sausage and crumble it. Heat 1 tbsp of oil and the sage in a non-stick frying pan. Add the sausage and fry briskly for 5 minutes, stirring constantly. Pour over the wine, bring to the boil and cook for about 5 minutes, only enough for the sausage meat to lose its raw colour.
2   While the sausage is cooking bring the stock to a simmer (keep it just simmering all through the cooking of the rice).
3   Heat the butter and remaining oil in a heavy-bottomed saucepan. Add the shallots and fry gently until soft and translucent – about 7 minutes.
4   Add the rice to the shallot *soffritto* and cook for 1–2 minutes, stirring constantly, until the grains are partly translucent.
5   Add the simmering stock a ladleful at a time. Wait to add another ladleful until the previous one has nearly all been absorbed.
6   Ten minutes after you start adding the stock, add the sausage and its juice to the rice. Stir well and continue cooking until the rice is al dente. Check the seasoning and serve at once, with the Parmesan handed round separately if you wish.

Some recipes for this dish, originally from Monza (now a suburb of Milan) suggest cutting the sausage in chunks and cooking it separately. In this case the sausage is also served separately and is added to the plated risotto by each diner. But in the following recipe, which I prefer, the fried sausage is added to the rice in the middle of the cooking so that the flavours of both ingredients blend thoroughly.
You need good 100% pure pork sausage.

Risotto alla Scozzese
RISOTTO WITH SMOKED SALMON AND WHISKY

Serves 4 as a first course
or 3 as a main course

60g unsalted butter
4 tbsp finely chopped shallot
sea salt
1.25 litres chicken
  or vegetable stock
300g Italian rice,
  preferably Carnaroli
4 tbsp Scotch whisky
225g smoked salmon,
  cut into 2cm pieces
5 tbsp double cream
2 tbsp chopped fresh dill
cayenne pepper
freshly grated Parmesan,
  to serve

1   Put the butter in a large, heavy-bottomed saucepan. Add the chopped shallot and a pinch of salt; this will release the moisture from the shallot thus preventing it from browning. Sauté until soft and translucent, about 7 minutes.

2   Meanwhile, in another saucepan heat the stock to simmering point (keep it simmering all through the cooking of the rice).

3   Add the rice to the shallot and stir to coat with butter, then cook for a couple of minutes, stirring constantly, until partly translucent. Add the whisky and let it bubble away, stirring constantly. Add a ladleful of simmering stock and cook the rice on a lively heat, adding a ladleful of stock whenever the rice begins to get dry.

4   When the rice is al dente, add the smoked salmon, cream, dill and cayenne pepper to taste. Mix thoroughly and check the salt before you transfer this delicious risotto to a heated dish. Serve at once, handing the cheese separately in a bowl for those who want it.

I love smoked salmon and, like most Italians, am not averse to an occasional glass of whisky. So here I have combined these two very Scottish ingredients with a favourite dish from my home country. This match with a Lombard risotto is particularly successful. The Parmesan is not necessary, but I think its flavour goes well with that of the smoked salmon.

Timballi e Pasticci di Riso
MOULDED AND BAKED
RICE DISHES

I have included a moulded dish recipe for this type of rice preparation. They are particularly suited to dinner parties, since they can be made in advance and then baked in the oven. They are dishes that need a more experienced cook, able to judge the exact cooking time of the different ingredients, and to shape and unmould the rice. A good point, however, is that cooked rice is very malleable. Should you find yourself with a *timballo tombé*, you can reshape the rice with your hands and nobody will know.

Torta di Risotto e Porri con la Salsa di Cozze

LEEK RISOTTO CAKE WITH MUSSEL SAUCE

Serves 6 as a first course
or 4 as a main course

1kg mussels
1 tbsp olive oil
2 garlic cloves
1 thick slice of lemon
350g leeks
1.25 litres vegetable stock
120g unsalted butter
450g Italian rice, preferably
 Vialone Nano
300ml dry white wine
sea salt and freshly ground
 black pepper
dried breadcrumbs for the dish
1 shallot, finely chopped
¼ tsp saffron strands

1   Scrub the mussels in a sink full of cold water, knock off the barnacles and tug off the beard. Rinse in several changes of cold water until the water is clean and no sand is left at the bottom of the sink. Discard any mussel that remains open after you have tapped it against a hard surface.

2   Put the oil, garlic and slice of lemon in a large sauté pan. Add the mussels, cover the pan and cook over a high heat until the mussels are open, about 4 minutes. Shake the pan very often.

3   Remove the mussel meat from the shells. Discard the shells and any mussel that remains closed. Pour the mussel liquid into a jug. Do it slowly so that you leave any sandy debris at the bottom of the pan. Set aside.

4   Cut off the green part of the leeks. Choose the best green leaves, wash them and blanch in boiling water for 2–3 minutes. Drain and cut into 1cm strips. Set aside.

5   Cut the white part of the leeks into very thin pieces. Wash thoroughly, drain and dry them.

6   Heat the stock in a saucepan until simmering (keep it simmering all through the making of the risotto).

7   Heat the oven to 180°C/Gas Mark 4.

8   Heat 60g of the butter and the white part of the leeks in a large heavy-bottomed saucepan. Sauté until the leeks are just soft and then mix in the rice. Sauté the rice until it is well coated with butter and the grains are partly translucent – about 2 minutes – and then pour over half the wine. Boil briskly for 1 minute, stirring constantly.

9   Add a ladleful of the simmering stock and stir well. As soon as nearly all the stock has been absorbed, add another ladleful of stock. Continue cooking the rice in this manner until it is very al dente, about 15 minutes. Mix in 30g of the butter. Taste and check the seasoning.

10   Very generously butter a 20cm soufflé dish or cake tin and coat it with the breadcrumbs. Spoon the risotto into it, press down gently and place in the oven while you prepare the sauce.

11   Put the shallot and remaining butter in a saucepan and sauté for 5 minutes.

12   Meanwhile, pound the saffron in a mortar. Add 2–3 tbsp of the mussel liquid, stir thoroughly and add to the shallot together with the remaining wine and mussel liquid. Bring slowly to the boil, and boil until it is reduced by about half. Add the mussels, stir and check the seasoning. You might have to add a little salt, and you need to add a lot of pepper. Cover the pan and draw off the heat.

13   Loosen the risotto from the mould with a palette knife. Turn the mould over onto a heated round platter, tap and shake and then lift it off. Drape the strips of the green part of the leeks over the risotto at regular intervals. Spoon a little of the mussel sauce over the top and pour the rest into a heated bowl. Serve immediately.

Leeks and mussels are complementary flavours. The rice here brings them together and gives substance to this dish. It is a fabulous dish for a party, well worth the time and effort.

Risotto coi Fegatini e i Funghi
RISOTTO WITH CHICKEN LIVERS AND PORCINI

Serves 6 as a first course
or 4–5 as a main course

For the sauce
30g dried porcini
30g unsalted butter
150g fresh chicken livers
60g fresh Italian sausage
 such as luganega, or
 Toulouse sausage, skinned
200g skinned and boned
 chicken breast, cut into
 bite-sized pieces
100g podded fresh young
 peas, or frozen petits pois
2 pinches of ground cloves
120ml red wine
sea salt and freshly ground
 black pepper

For the risotto
60g unsalted butter
2 tbsp finely chopped onion
1 tbsp finely chopped celery
1 tbsp finely chopped carrot
400g Italian rice, preferably
 Carnaroli or Arborio
1 tbsp tomato purée
120ml red wine
1.5 litres chicken stock
sea salt and freshly ground
 black pepper
6 tbsp freshly grated
 Parmesan

1 Soak the dried porcini in very hot water for 30 minutes. Lift them out, rinse them and dry them. Chop them coarsely. Filter the porcini liquid through a sieve lined with muslin.

2 Heat the butter in a small saucepan. Add the porcini and cook gently for about 10 minutes.

3 Meanwhile, clean the chicken livers, removing all the fat and gristle. Cut into bite-sized pieces and put in a small saucepan with the sausage, chicken and peas. Add the cloves, wine, and salt and pepper to taste. Bring to the boil and cook, uncovered, for about 10 minutes, stirring very frequently. Mix in the porcini with all their juices and continue cooking for a further 10 minutes. Taste to check the seasoning. Set aside, and reheat before serving.

4 To make the risotto, first bring the stock to a simmer (keep it just simmering all through the cooking of the rice).

5 Heat half the butter with the onion, celery and carrot in a wide heavy-bottomed saucepan. Cook gently until the vegetables are soft, about 10 minutes, stirring very frequently.

6 Heat the oven to 170°C/Gas Mark 3.

7 Mix the rice into the vegetables and sauté for a minute or so until the grains are partly translucent. Stir in the tomato purée, cook for 30 seconds and then pour in the wine. Boil rapidly for 1 minute, stirring constantly.

8 Add a ladleful of the simmering stock and 2–3 tbsp of the porcini liquid. Cook the risotto, gradually adding the remaining stock in the usual way.

When the risotto is nearly done and still on the liquid side, draw off the heat. Taste and add salt and pepper. Mix in the rest of the butter and the Parmesan. Cover the pan and leave until the butter has melted, and then mix thoroughly.

9 Ladle the risotto into a bowl, spoon the sauce all over it and serve immediately.

Risi Asciutti e Minestre di Riso
RICE AND VEGETABLE DISHES AND RICE SOUPS

The first 2 recipes in this section are for dishes that are midway between a soup and a risotto. The rice is boiled in the stock in which the vegetables are cooking, thus the dishes are definitely not risotti. This method of cooking ensures that the taste of the vegetable predominates over the flavour of the rice.

The last 3 recipes are for soups, all from my home town, Milan, the motherland of good soups. Rice soup is very popular, and this can vary from a rich earthy minestrone to a sophisticated soup with pieces of chicken and grains of rice and almonds floating in a pale blond pool – a very Chinese-looking soup.

Riso con le Verdure
RICE WITH VEGETABLES

Serves 6 as a first course
or 4 as a main course

1 large waxy potato, diced
2 carrots, diced
1 large leek, white and green
 part, cut into rounds
120g podded fresh peas
 or green beans, according
 to season
1 celery stick, diced
1 courgette, diced
sea salt and freshly ground
 black pepper
300g Italian rice, preferably
 Vialone Nano
100ml extra virgin olive oil
3 garlic cloves, finely chopped
12 fresh sage leaves, chopped
2 large ripe tomatoes, peeled,
 seeded and coarsely chopped
120g Italian fontina or
 raclette, diced
6 tbsp freshly grated
 Parmesan

1   Choose a large pot – I use my earthenware stockpot with a 5-litre capacity. Put all the washed and cut vegetables in it and add enough water to come three-quarters of the way up the side of the pot. Season with salt, bring to the boil and simmer, uncovered, for 20–25 minutes.
2   Add the rice to the vegetables, stir well and cook for about 15 minutes or until done. The vegetables should be nice and soft and the rice should be al dente, thus giving a pleasing contrast of texture.
3   While the rice is cooking, make a little *soffritto* (frying mixture). Heat the oil, garlic and sage in a small frying pan until the sage begins to sizzle and the aroma of the garlic to rise. Add the tomatoes and cook for 5 minutes, stirring occasionally.
4   When the rice is ready, drain the contents of the stockpot very well (you can keep the liquid for a soup) and transfer the rice and vegetable mixture, a ladleful at a time, into a serving bowl. Dress each ladleful with a couple of spoonfuls of the *soffritto*, a handful of cheese cubes, a generous grinding of pepper and a spoonful of Parmesan. Mix very thoroughly after each addition, and serve at once.
Note: By dressing the dish gradually you make sure that the *soffritto* and the cheese are equally distributed.

Northern and southern Italy meet happily in this dish, which was given to me by the Neapolitan owner of a superb greengrocer in Valtellina, an Alpine valley north of Milan. The dish is halfway between a minestrone and a risotto with vegetables and yet it tastes different from both. The flavour of the vegetables comes through strongly, enhanced by the final *soffritto*.

Risi e Bisi
RICE WITH PEAS

Serves 4–6 as a first course

1 small onion, very finely
 chopped
45g unsalted butter
1 tbsp olive oil
700g young fresh peas, podded
1.5 litres chicken stock
250g Italian rice,
 preferably Vialone Nano
1 tsp fennel seeds, crushed,
 or 2 tbsp chopped flat-leaf
 parsley
75g Parmesan, freshly grated
sea salt and freshly ground
 black pepper

1 Put the onion, half the butter and the oil in a heavy-bottomed saucepan and sauté until the onion is pale golden and soft. Mix in the peas and cook over a low heat for 10 minutes, adding a few spoonfuls of stock during the cooking.

2 Meanwhile, bring the remaining stock to the boil in another saucepan.

3 Add the rice to the peas and sauté for 2 minutes, turning the rice over and over until the grains are partly translucent. Now pour over the boiling stock. Stir well and bring back to the boil. Simmer gently, stirring occasionally, until the rice is al dente. You might have to add a little more stock during the cooking.

4 A few minutes before the rice is done, add the fennel seeds or parsley, the rest of the butter and 4 tbsp of the Parmesan. Taste and add salt and pepper to your liking. Stir thoroughly and finish the cooking, then serve at once with the rest of the cheese handed round separately.

The Venetians' love of rice and peas is sublimated in this, the most aristocratic of rice dishes. It was served at the Doge's banquets on the feast of San Marco, 25 April, when the first young peas, grown on the islands of the Venetian lagoon, appear in the market. This is the old recipe, in which fennel seeds are used instead of parsley. The best rice to use for the dish is Vialone Nano.

Riso e Lenticchie
RICE WITH LENTILS

Serves 4–5

4 tbsp olive oil

1 small onion, very finely
  chopped

60g smoked pancetta, cut into
  tiny pieces

1 small carrot

1 large celery stick

1 sprig of fresh rosemary,
  about 5cm long

1 garlic clove

sea salt and freshly ground
  black pepper

1 heaped tsp tomato purée

1.5 litres vegetable stock,
  or 2 vegetable stock cubes
  dissolved in the same amount
  of water

200g green lentils, rinsed and
  drained

200g Italian rice, preferably
  Vialone Nano

extra virgin olive oil for the
  table, a Tuscan or Roman oil

1 Heat the oil, onion and pancetta in a heavy-bottomed saucepan.
(I use an earthenware pot when I cook pulses.) Sauté for about 7 minutes,
stirring frequently. The onion must become soft but not coloured.

2 Chop together finely the carrot, celery, rosemary leaves and garlic.
Add to the onion *soffritto* – frying mixture – and cook at low heat for
about 10 minutes. Stir frequently. Season with salt and stir in the tomato
purée. Cook for a further minute.

3 Meanwhile, heat the stock in a separate saucepan.

4 Add the lentils to the vegetable mixture. Stir well and let them
insaporire – take up the flavour – for a minute or two.

5 Pour enough stock into the pan to cover the lentils by about 5cm.
Place a lid over the saucepan and cook until the lentils are soft, not al
dente. It is difficult to say how long that will take since it depends on the
quality and freshness of the pulses. Usually lentils are ready within 1 hour.
Check the liquid every now and then and add more stock whenever the
lentils are too dry.

6 Add the rest of the stock and bring back to the boil. Mix in the rice
and, if necessary, add more boiling stock. If you have used all the stock,
pour in boiling water. The amount of liquid needed varies with the quality
of the lentils, the kind of rice used and the heat on which the soup is
cooked. The resulting soup should be quite thick: lots of rice and lentils
in a little liquid.

7 Season with lots of pepper, and simmer until the rice is al dente
(15–20 minutes).

8 Taste and adjust the seasoning. Serve the soup straight away, handing
round a bottle of extra virgin olive oil for everyone to pour a little over his
serving of soup. Although not essential, I recommend this last *battesimo* –
christening – because the oil livens up the earthy soup with its fruity flavour.

This is an earthy, nourishing soup, which I first had one
lunchtime in Rome in a busy, bustling trattoria opposite
the Quirinale. It was the most lively place imaginable,
crowded with civil servants enjoying good, homely
Roman food.

Minestra di Riso, Mandorle e Prezzemolo

RICE, ALMOND AND PARSLEY SOUP

Serves 4

120g peeled almonds
1.25 litres chicken stock
1 chicken breast on the bone
120g Italian rice, preferably
  Vialone Nano
3 tbsp chopped flat-leaf parsley
sea salt and freshly ground
  black pepper

1   Heat the oven to 220°C/Gas Mark 7.
2   Place the almonds on a baking tray and bake for 10 minutes, or until the aroma rises and the almonds are golden. Chop them to the size of grains of rice.
3   In a large saucepan heat the stock until boiling. Put in the chicken breast and cook gently for 10 minutes. Lift the breast out of the stock and place on a board. Add the rice to the stock, and mix in.
4   While the rice is cooking, skin and bone the chicken breast and cut the meat into small strips.
5   When the rice is nearly done, stir in the chicken strips, almonds and parsley and continue cooking until the rice is ready. Taste and add salt if necessary, and pepper. Ladle the soup into hot bowls.

No clear soup like this can be successful without the basis of a good home-made stock. If you haven't got some chicken stock ready in the freezer, you can make it with a good-quality chicken bouillon cube, of which there are quite a few on the market.
This is a delicate soup to be given to people who appreciate the balance of good ingredients.

Minestrone alla Milanese
VEGETABLE SOUP WITH RICE

Serves 6

2 tbsp olive oil
30g butter
120g unsmoked pancetta,
 or unsmoked streaky bacon,
 chopped
2 onions, coarsely chopped
4 or 5 fresh sage leaves,
 snipped
1 tbsp chopped flat-leaf parsley
2 garlic cloves, chopped
2 carrots, diced
2 celery sticks, diced
2 potatoes, about 225g, diced
120g green beans,
 cut into 2cm pieces
225g courgettes, diced
225g Italian canned plum
 tomatoes with their juice
sea salt and freshly ground
 black pepper
225g Savoy cabbage,
 cut into strips
150g Italian rice, preferably
 Semifino Padano or
 Vialone Nano
400g canned borlotti beans,
 drained
freshly grated Parmesan,
 to serve

1 Heat the oil and butter in a stockpot or a large saucepan, add the pancetta and sauté for 2 minutes. Add the onions, sage and parsley and fry gently for 5 minutes or so.

2 Mix in the garlic, carrots, celery and potatoes and fry for 2 minutes. Add the green beans and courgettes and sauté for a further couple of minutes.

3 Cover with 2.5 litres of hot water and add the tomatoes and salt and pepper to taste. Cover the pan and cook at a very low simmer for a minimum of 1½ hours. Minestrone can be cooked for as long as 3 hours and it will be even better. Do not think that the vegetables will break; they do not.

4 About 30 minutes before you want to eat, add the cabbage and cook for 15 minutes. Then add the rice and the canned beans and stir well. Continue cooking uncovered at a steady simmer until the rice is al dente. Serve with a bowl of Parmesan on the side.

This is the classic minestrone with rice, where rice is the starchy nourishment added to a vegetable soup. Minestrone is even better made a day in advance and warmed up. In the summer it is delicious cold, though not straight from the fridge.

Ripieni e Insalate di Riso
RICE STUFFINGS AND SALADS

Two recipes for rice stuffings hardly do justice to an array of dishes in which rice is the primary ingredient of the stuffing. But I have chosen my favourites.

While rice is commonly used as a stuffing for vegetables, its use in stuffing fish is less usual. The recipe for squid stuffed with rice is very interesting and very good; in fact, it is my preferred way of stuffing squid.

The versatility of rice is boundless. It even makes excellent salads, which is more than can be said for pasta. I have also included in this section two of my favourite recipes for rice salads.

Pomodori Ripieni di Riso
TOMATOES STUFFED WITH BASIL-FLAVOURED RICE

Serves 4 as a first course

450g ripe tomatoes,
 all the same size
sea salt and freshly ground
 black pepper
90g Italian rice, preferably
 Vialone Nano
2 garlic cloves, finely sliced
12 fresh basil leaves, snipped
1 egg
100ml extra virgin olive oil

1 Wash and dry the tomatoes. Cut them across in half. Scoop out some of the seeds and discard. Scoop out all the pulp and the juice with a pointed spoon, taking care not to break the skin. Chop the pulp and put it in a bowl with the juice.

2 Sprinkle the insides of the tomato halves with salt and place them in the fridge for at least 30 minutes.

3 Add the rice to the bowl together with the garlic and basil.

4 Beat the egg very lightly and mix thoroughly into the rice mixture. Add the oil, plenty of pepper and salt to taste. Mix again very well and leave for at least 3 hours.

5 Heat the oven to 190°C/Gas Mark 5.

6 Oil a large oven dish and place the tomato halves in it, cut side up. Fill them with the rice mixture, to come level with the tops of the tomatoes. Cover the dish with foil and bake until the rice is cooked, about 45 minutes. Serve hot.

The rice in this recipe is not previously cooked, but only soaked in oil so that it retains a stronger flavour. By the end of the cooking the tomatoes are very soft and become amalgamated with the rice, rather than being separate containers.

Calamari Ripieni di Riso
SQUID STUFFED WITH RICE

Serves 3–4 as a main course

4 large squid, about 1kg
6 tbsp olive oil
4 level tbsp cooked Italian rice,
  preferably Vialone Nano
3 tbsp chopped flat-leaf parsley
2 garlic cloves, chopped
½–1 dried chilli, chopped
grated zest of ½ organic lemon
2 salted anchovies, boned and
  rinsed, or 4 canned anchovy
  fillets, drained
sea salt and freshly ground
  black pepper
120ml dry white wine

Rice, a staple of the north, is sometimes used in fish dishes in Puglia, the heel of the Italian boot. The fish used there for this dish is cuttlefish. Although this is a fairly common species off the south coast of England, most of the best catch is shipped straight to France and Spain. For this reason I prefer to use squid, which are easily available. Whenever I can, I buy the local squid, which are better than the imported squid from the Mediterranean.

1 Ask your fishmonger to clean the squid, or do it yourself by following these instructions. Hold the sac in one hand and pull off the tentacles with the other hand. The contents of the sac will come out too. Cut the tentacles above the eyes. Squeeze out the thin bony beak in the centre of the tentacles. Peel off the skin from the sac and the flap. Remove the translucent backbone from inside the sac and rinse the sac and tentacles under cold water. Keep the sacs whole.

2 Cut the tentacles into small pieces and then chop them coarsely until they are about the same size as the grains of rice.

3 Put 2 tbsp of the oil in a sauté pan. Add the rice, chopped tentacles, parsley, garlic, chilli and lemon zest and sauté briskly for a few minutes to *insaporire* – let the mixture take up all the flavours.

4 Finely chop the anchovy fillets and stir into the mixture. Cook at a lower temperature for a minute or so. Taste and add salt and pepper, if necessary.

5 Heat the oven to 180°C/Gas Mark 4.

6 Fill each squid sac with the rice mixture. Do not pack the stuffing too tight or the sac will burst during the cooking. Stitch up the opening with a needle and thread and lay the squid in a single layer, close to each other, in an oven dish. (I use a metal tin, because metal transmits the heat better than ceramic.)

Recipe continued overleaf

SQUID STUFFED WITH RICE

continued

7 Pour the rest of the oil and the wine over the squid. Cover the oven dish tightly with a piece of foil and bake for about 1 hour, until the squid are tender when pricked with a fork.

8 When they are done, transfer the squid to a carving board and allow to cool for 10 minutes. Slice off a very thin strip from the sewn end to eliminate the thread. Cut each sac into thick slices of about 2.5cm. If you possess one, use an electric carving knife which will make this slicing very easy. Otherwise see that your knife is very sharp. Gently transfer the slices to a serving dish.

9 Taste the cooking juices. If bland, boil briskly until reduced and full of flavour. Spoon over the squid. You can serve the dish hot, warm or even at room temperature, which I personally prefer.

Riso e Ceci in Insalata
RICE AND CHICKPEA SALAD

Serves 4

150g dried chickpeas, or
  400g canned or organic
  chickpeas (in cartons)
sea salt and freshly ground
  black pepper
1 tsp bicarbonate of soda
1 tbsp flour
1 small onion, cut in half
1 celery stick, cut in half
2 sprigs of fresh rosemary
4 fresh sage leaves
a few parsley stalks
2 garlic cloves
7 tbsp extra virgin olive oil
200g Italian rice, preferably
  Vialone Nano or Semifino
  Padano
1 garlic clove, finely chopped
a lovely bunch of fresh flat-leaf
  parsley, finely chopped
225g best ripe tomatoes,
  peeled and seeded
12 fresh basil leaves, snipped

It is surprising how two ingredients as modest as rice and chickpeas can produce, when mixed together, such a really good and attractive dish.

Cook the chickpeas properly until they are soft. In common with my compatriots, I find nothing more unpleasant than undercooked pulses, as they are sometimes served in 'Britalian' restaurants. The rice should be al dente, not because of the overpraised 'contrast of texture', but simply because rice is good al dente. Chickpeas, however, are good when soft. I usually use dried chickpeas, which I soak overnight before cooking. These are far better than the canned ones. But should you prefer to cut out the soaking and cooking, I suggest you use the organic chickpeas that come in cartons.

Recipe continued overleaf

RICE AND CHICKPEA SALAD

continued

1   Put the chickpeas in a large bowl and cover with plenty of cold water. Mix the salt, bicarbonate of soda and flour with a little cold water to make a paste and stir this into the soaking water. This helps to tenderise the skin as well as the chickpeas themselves. Leave to soak for at least 18 hours; 24 is better.

2   Rinse the chickpeas and put them in a pot. (An earthenware stockpot is the best for cooking pulses because of earthenware's heat-retaining properties.) Add the onion and celery and cover with water to come about 8cm over the chickpeas. Place the pot on the heat.

3   Tie the rosemary, sage, parsley stalks and whole garlic cloves in a small piece of muslin to make a bundle and add to the pot. Bring to the boil, then lower the heat and cook, covered, until the chickpeas are ready. The liquid should simmer rather than boil. Chickpeas take 2–3 hours to cook. Add salt only when they are nearly done, as the salt tends to make the skin crack and wrinkle.

4   Drain the chickpeas (you can keep the liquid for a bean or vegetable soup). Fish out and discard the onion, celery and herb bag. Transfer the chickpeas to a bowl and toss, while still hot, with 2 tbsp of the oil.

5   Cook the rice in plenty of boiling salted water. Drain when just al dente. Mix into the chickpeas.

6   Put the rest of the oil, the chopped garlic and chopped parsley in a small frying pan. Sauté for 2 minutes, stirring constantly.

7   Dice the tomatoes and mix into the *soffritto* – frying mixture. Cook for 1 minute and then spoon over the rice and chickpea mixture. Add the snipped fresh basil and plenty of pepper. Toss thoroughly but lightly. Taste and check the salt. Serve at room temperature.

Insalata di Riso con Mozzarella ed Acciughe
RICE SALAD WITH MOZZARELLA AND ANCHOVY FILLETS

Serves 4 as a first course

250g Italian rice,
 preferably Vialone Nano
sea salt and freshly ground
 black pepper
6 tbsp extra virgin olive oil
2 hard-boiled eggs
150g buffalo mozzarella,
 cut into small cubes
6 salted anchovies, boned and
 rinsed, or 12 canned anchovy
 fillets, drained
4 tbsp chopped flat-leaf
 parsley
1 small garlic clove, very
 finely chopped
1 small dried chilli, seeded
 and crumbled
12 black olives
1 tbsp capers, rinsed and dried

1   Cook the rice in plenty of boiling salted water until just al dente. (Remember that when served cold, rice is better if a touch undercooked.) Drain the rice, rinse under cold water and drain again. Transfer the rice to a bowl and pat dry with kitchen paper. Add 2 tbsp of the oil and set aside to cool.

2   Chop the eggs and add to the rice, together with the mozzarella.

3   Chop the anchovy fillets and place in another bowl. Mix in the parsley, garlic and chilli. Beat in the remaining oil with a fork until the sauce thickens. Season with salt and pepper to taste.

4   Spoon this dressing into the rice and mix very thoroughly with 2 forks so as to separate all the grains. Taste and adjust the seasoning to your liking. Scatter the olives and capers here and there and serve cold, but not chilled.

I strongly recommend using buffalo mozzarella for this dish. If possible, dress the rice 2 hours before serving.

Risi Dolci
SWEET RICE DISHES

These last three rice recipes do not originate from the
northern regions of Italy as do all the previous ones.
The rice cake and rice fritters are from Tuscany and the
Black Rice Pudding is, oddly enough, from Sicily.

Torta di Riso
RICE CAKE WITH ALMONDS AND SULTANAS

Serves 8

750ml full-fat milk
180g golden caster sugar
strip of organic lemon zest,
  yellow part only
2.5cm piece of vanilla pod
5cm piece of cinnamon stick
sea salt
75g Italian rice,
  preferably Arborio
4 tbsp sultanas
2 tbsp dark rum
100g peeled almonds
4 large eggs, separated
grated zest of ½ organic lemon
butter and dried breadcrumbs
  for the tin
icing sugar, to finish

*This is the Florentine version
of a cake that is popular all over
central Italy. I make it with
Arborio rice, as it swells during
the cooking while absorbing
the milk. You can add other
ingredients to taste, for
instance chocolate pieces
and/or candied peel. It is a firm
yet moist cake, not a pudding,
that is equally delicious with
or without a dollop of thick
cream on top. It should not
be served until at least the
day after making, to allow
the flavours to blend.*

1 Put the milk, 30g of the sugar, the strip of lemon zest, the vanilla pod, cinnamon stick and a pinch of salt in a saucepan and bring to the boil. Add the rice and stir well with a wooden spoon. Cook, uncovered, over a very low heat for about 35 minutes, stirring frequently, until the rice has absorbed the milk and is soft. Set aside to cool.

2 Heat the oven to 180°C/Gas Mark 4.

3 Put the sultanas in a bowl and pour over the rum. Leave them to puff up.

4 Spread the almonds on a baking tray and toast them in the oven for about 10 minutes or until they are quite brown. Shake the tray occasionally to prevent them from burning. Cool them a little, then chop them coarsely.

5 Remove the strip of lemon zest, the vanilla pod and cinnamon stick from the rice and spoon the rice into a mixing bowl. (Wash and dry the vanilla pod so that you can use it again.) Add the egg yolks, one at a time, mixing well after each addition. Add the remaining sugar, the almonds, sultanas with the rum and the grated lemon zest to the rice and egg mixture and mix everything together thoroughly.

6 Whisk the egg whites until they are stiff, then fold them gently into the rice mixture.

7 Butter a 20cm springform tin. Line the bottom with baking paper and then butter the paper. Sprinkle all over with breadcrumbs to coat evenly, and shake out the excess crumbs.

8 Spoon the rice mixture into the prepared tin. Bake in the oven (still at the same temperature) for about 45 minutes or until a thin skewer or a wooden cocktail stick inserted in the middle of the cake comes out just moist. The cake should also have shrunk a little from the sides of the tin.

9 Leave the cake to cool in the tin, then remove the clipped band and turn the cake over onto a plate. Remove the base of the tin and the lining paper. Place a round serving platter on the cake and turn it over again. Leave for at least 24 hours before serving the cake. Sprinkle with sifted icing sugar before serving.

Riso Nero
BLACK RICE PUDDING

Serves 6

600ml full-fat milk
75g Italian rice
100g caster sugar
100g peeled almonds, chopped
pinch of sea salt
pinch of ground cinnamon
150ml black coffee
50g bitter chocolate
 (70% cocoa solids), flaked
 or grated
grated zest of 1 small organic
 orange
15g unsalted butter
150ml whipping cream

1 Put the milk, rice, sugar, almonds, salt, cinnamon and coffee in a heavy-bottomed saucepan. Bring to the boil and simmer until the rice is very soft, about 1 hour, stirring frequently. If you use a flame diffuser you can leave it a little longer, but be careful because the milky rice tends to stick to the bottom of the pan.

2 Draw the pan off the heat and mix in the chocolate and the orange zest.

3 Grease a 900ml pudding basin with the butter. Spoon in the rice mixture and leave to cool. When cold, cover with cling film and put in the fridge to chill.

4 Free the pudding all round with a palette knife and turn it out onto a round platter.

5 Whip the cream and spread it all over the brown dome just before serving.

There are not many rice dishes in Sicily, but this is one of the few Sicilian contributions to the vast range of Italian rice sweets. It is different from the rice desserts of the central Italian regions – the motherland of rice cakes and puddings – because it contains a high proportion of chocolate and coffee.

In Sicily this dish is served without cream, but even though I am not a cream fan, I must admit that cream lightens the almondy chocolate flavour of the riso nero.

Frittelle di Riso
RICE FRITTERS

Serves 4

600ml full-fat milk
pinch of sea salt
75g Italian rice, preferably
 Semifino Padano or
 Vialone Nano
2 tbsp sugar
pared zest of ½ organic
 orange, in strips
pared zest of ½ organic lemon,
 in strips
2 large eggs
vegetable oil for frying
icing sugar, to decorate

1 Put the milk, salt, rice, sugar and fruit zest in a heavy-bottomed saucepan. Bring slowly to the boil, stirring frequently. Cook, uncovered, at a very low heat for about 1 hour or until the rice has absorbed all the milk and is very soft. Stir frequently. Spoon the mixture into a bowl and allow to cool a little.
2 Lightly beat the eggs to break the white, then incorporate into the rice mixture. Mix very well and place the bowl in the fridge. If possible chill for 1 hour so the mixture firms, which will make it easier to shape and fry.
3 Heat the oil to 170°C in a wok or a frying pan. At this temperature a piece of stale bread should brown in 50 seconds.
4 Discard the orange and lemon zest from the rice mixture. With a metal spoon pick up some of the rice mixture – a dollop about the size of a large walnut – and with the help of a second spoon slide it into the oil. Fry the fritters in batches until they are golden on both sides. Retrieve them with a fish slice and place on kitchen paper to drain.
5 Sprinkle each fritter very generously with sifted icing sugar before serving. They are good hot or cold.

These fritters are sold and eaten in the streets of Florence and other Italian towns as a *merenda* – snack – and they are absolutely delicious. You can easily make them yourself and try to recapture the atmosphere of your Italian holidays.

'Il vero lusso di una mensa sta nel dessert'
'The real luxury of a meal lies in the dessert.'

From *Il Piacere* by
GABRIELE D'ANNUNZIO

DOLCI

Italians love sweets, although they only eat them on special occasions. An everyday meal ends with fresh fruit; sweets are kept for Sundays, parties, family gatherings, religious days and village *feste*.

Dolci developed differently in northern, central and southern Italy. The dolci of the north are often little more than sweet breads, the panettone milanese being the prime example. The dolci of central Italy are richer, with lots of spices, nuts, candied peel and honey, as in the panforte from Siena or the *certosino* from Bologna. It was also in this part of the country that there originated the '*dolci al cucchiaio*' (sweets that can be eaten with a spoon such as the *zuppe inglesi*, or trifles) of Emilia-Romagna and Tuscany. In southern Italy the protagonists of dolci are almonds and candied fruits, a heritage from Arab cooking. And it is here that dolci reach the highest level of culinary art.

This being Italy, there are, of course, many exceptions to this rule. After all, the birthplace of zabaglione – the *dolce al cucchiaio* par excellence – is Piedmont in the north, while a *ciambella* – sweet ring-shaped bread made with potatoes, eggs and flour – is a traditional dolce of Puglia.

As they are eaten on feast days, dolci are even more regional than other kinds of food. Every patron saint, every feast day of the year, has its own special dolce, in every town in Italy. The region that has more special occasions, and more legends, associated with its dolci is Sicily. There are biscuits called *frutti di morte* – fruits of death – made with *pasta reale* – almond paste – that are eaten at the end of a meal on All Souls' Day, 2 November. The *sfinci di San Giuseppe* are a sort of fritter eaten on St Joseph's Day, 19 March. For Easter Sunday a magnificent *agnello pasquale* – Easter lamb – is made in Sicily with a pastry, strongly flavoured with cloves, that is moulded in the shape of a lamb.

Some of these special dolci have become so popular that they are now eaten all year round, not only in Italy but elsewhere, as is the case with panettone and panforte, both originally eaten only at Christmas. Others are still very localised and known only in the place where they are made. When I was in Sicily some years ago I ate some superb soft biscuits called *olivette di Sant'Agata*. They were made of marzipan, sugar, rum and vanilla, and are a speciality of Catania, made originally on the saint's day of Sant'Agata, a local martyr. I had never heard of *olivette* before, yet they are the best almond-based sweets I have ever had. Our Sicilian hostess insisted that we drive many, many miles along the motorway to an old-fashioned *pasticceria* in Catania to buy 'the only *olivette* worth eating'. The lengths Italians will go in their search for excellence, as far as food is concerned, never ceases to amaze me.

The tradition of excellence in Italian dolci goes back a long way. Writing in Naples at the beginning of the nineteenth century, Lady Blessington, a friend of Emma Hamilton, commented, 'Italian confectionery and ices are far superior to those of the French and the English, and their variety is infinite.' A passage from *Il Gattopardo* by Giuseppe Tomasi di Lampedusa gives a good idea of what Lady Blessington meant. He describes how, at the great ball, 'the table was covered with pink parfaits, champagne parfaits, grey parfaits which parted creaking under the blade of the cake knife; a violin melody in major of candied morello cherries; acid notes of yellow pineapples; and the *trionfi della gola* – triumphs of gluttony – with the opaque green of their pistachio paste, and the shameless *minni di virgini* – virgins' breasts' – dome-shaped pastry cupcakes stuffed with ricotta, chocolate pieces and candied fruits and with a candied cherry stuck on the top.

Torte e Crostate
CAKES AND TARTS

The emphasis of this section is on cakes containing fruit and nuts.

In Italy, cakes, even the drier sort, are often eaten as part of a meal. Cakes are also served mid-morning or after supper, when they are traditionally accompanied by a glass of wine. Wine, after all, used to be the cheapest beverage, one that even poor people in the country could afford. They made their own wine, while tea or coffee had to be bought.

In all the cake and biscuit recipes, I recommend the use of Italian 00 flour. This is a high-quality flour with very little flavour and very good raising properties. It is available from most supermarkets and delicatessens.

Torta di Polenta
POLENTA CAKE

Serves about 8

120g peeled almonds
125g unsalted butter, cut into
 small lumps and softened
125g golden caster sugar
75g plain flour or
 Italian 00 flour
100g coarse polenta flour
2 tsp baking powder
pinch of sea salt
2 eggs plus 2 egg yolks
grated zest of 1 organic lemon
unsalted butter and dried
 breadcrumbs for the tin
icing sugar, to decorate

1   Heat the oven to 180°C/Gas Mark 4.
2   Spread the almonds on a baking tray and toast them in the oven for about 10 minutes, or until they begin to turn golden. Remove the tray from the oven, but leave the oven on.
3   Put the almonds in the bowl of a food processor and blitz until they are ground, but be careful not to reduce them to powder.
4   Beat together the butter and the sugar until creamy. In a bowl mix together the flours, baking powder and the salt and then add to the butter and cream mix. Lightly beat together the eggs and egg yolks and slowly add to the flour mixture, while beating the whole time. Mix in the lemon zest.
5   Butter a 23cm loaf tin and spread about 2 tbsp of dried breadcrumbs all over the buttered surface and then shake off the excess crumbs.
6   Spoon the cake mixture into the tin and bake for about 45 minutes, or until a skewer inserted into the centre of the cake comes out clean. When the cake is cooked, it will have shrunk from the sides of the tin and be quite springy to the touch.
7   Loosen the cake all around the tin with a palette knife, invert the tin onto a wire rack and leave the cake to cool. Just before you want to eat it, sprinkle sifted icing sugar over the top.

In this peasant cake from the region of Veneto, polenta flour is used together with white flour to give the cake a more grainy texture. Try to get the coarse polenta flour, which is available in some supermarkets and in Italian delicatessens. For the same reason, you *must*, if at all possible, grind the almonds yourself, instead of buying already ground almonds that are too powdery.

Torta di Cioccolato con le Pere
CHOCOLATE AND PEAR CAKE

Serves 4–6

75g bitter chocolate
  (70% cocoa solids),
  broken into small pieces
75g unsalted butter, at room
  temperature
100g icing sugar, sifted
2 eggs, at room temperature,
  separated
1 egg yolk, at room
  temperature
2 pinches ground cinnamon
pinch of sea salt
120g plain flour or
  Italian 00 flour
200–250g firm ripe pears,
  peeled and cut into
  1cm pieces
unsalted butter and dried
  breadcrumbs for the tin
icing sugar, to decorate

1   Heat the oven to 130°C/Gas Mark ½. Put the chocolate in a heatproof bowl and melt it in the oven. Remove from the oven and keep in a warm place. Turn the oven heat up to 180°C/Gas Mark 4.

2   Beat the butter until really soft. I use a hand-held electric mixer. Gradually add the icing sugar while beating constantly, then beat until light and pale yellow. (If you add all the sugar at once and start beating butter and sugar together, you will find the sugar flying everywhere except in the butter.) Add the 3 egg yolks, cinnamon, salt and melted chocolate.

3   Whisk the 2 egg whites until stiff but not dry and then fold into the mixture by the spoonful, alternating with spoonfuls of flour. Fold lightly but thoroughly.

4   Lightly mix the pear pieces into the mixture.

5   Butter a 23cm loaf tin and sprinkle in the dried breadcrumbs. Shake the tin so the crumbs cover all the buttered surface and then turn the tin upside down and throw away the excess crumbs. Spoon the cake mixture into the tin. Bake for about 50 minutes or until the sides of the cake have shrunk from the tin and the cake is dry in the middle – test by inserting a wooden cocktail stick.

6   Remove the tin from the oven, unmould the cake onto a wire rack and leave to cool.

7   Sprinkle with sifted icing sugar just before serving.

I make this cake in a loaf tin, as it used to be made at my home in Milan for our *merenda* – afternoon tea. If you want to serve it as a dessert, I suggest making it in a 15cm round tin and serve it with either whipping or pouring cream, whatever you prefer.

Torta di Noci
WALNUT CAKE

Serves 6–8

120g unsalted butter, at room
  temperature
180g icing sugar, sifted
3 large eggs, at room
  temperature, separated
150g walnut pieces
120g plain flour or
  Italian 00 flour
½ tbsp baking powder
pinch of sea salt
grated zest of 1 organic lemon
¼ tsp lemon juice
unsalted butter and dried
  breadcrumbs for the tin
icing sugar, to decorate

1   Heat the oven to 180°C/Gas Mark 4.
2   Beat the butter until very soft. Gradually beat in the icing sugar to make a smooth thick cream. Use a hand-held electric mixer, if you have one.
3   Lightly beat the egg yolks together with a fork, then add gradually to the butter cream, mixing thoroughly to incorporate.
4   Put the walnuts in a food processor and process until very coarsely ground while pulsing the machine. The nuts should be grainy, not ground fine. Stir into the butter mixture.
5   Sift the flour, baking powder and salt together and fold into the butter mixture with the lemon zest.
6   Whisk the egg whites with the lemon juice until stiff but not dry and fold into the mixture, using a metal spoon and lifting it high to incorporate more air.
7   Generously butter a 20cm springform cake tin. Sprinkle with breadcrumbs, shake the tin to cover all the surface and then shake out the excess crumbs. Spoon the cake mixture into the prepared tin.
8   Bake for about 45 minutes, or until the cake is done. Test by inserting a wooden cocktail stick into the middle of the cake; it should come out dry. Unclip the side band and turn the cake over onto a wire rack to cool.
9   Sprinkle lavishly with sifted icing sugar before serving.

Buy your walnuts from a shop with a quick turnover so that they will not be old and rancid. Better still, buy the nuts in their shells at Christmas time and shell them yourself. Keep them in the freezer.

Torta di Ricotta
RICOTTA CAKE

Serves 10–12

120g sultanas
300g caster sugar
120g unsalted butter,
 at room temperature
4 large eggs,
 at room temperature
grated zest of 1 organic lemon
6 tbsp potato flour
1 tbsp baking powder
½ tsp sea salt
1kg fresh ricotta
unsalted butter for the tin
icing sugar, to decorate

1　Soak the sultanas in hot water for 15 minutes to puff them up.
2　Reserve 1 tbsp of the caster sugar. Beat the butter with the remaining caster sugar until pale and creamy and then add the eggs, one at a time. When all the eggs have been incorporated, mix in the lemon zest, potato flour, baking powder and salt.
3　Heat the oven to 180°C/Gas Mark 4.
4　Press the ricotta through the small-hole disc of a food mill, or through a sieve, directly onto the other ingredients. Do not use a food processor as this would not aerate the ricotta. Fold the ricotta thoroughly into the mixture. Drain the sultanas, pat them dry with kitchen paper and fold into the mixture.
5　Generously butter a 25cm springform cake tin and sprinkle with the reserved caster sugar to coat the bottom and sides.
6　Spoon the ricotta mixture into the tin and bake for 1–1¼ hours or until the cake is done (it will shrink slightly from the sides of the tin). Leave to cool in the tin. Unmould the cake when cold and place on a flat serving dish. Sprinkle with plenty of sifted icing sugar just before serving.

I do believe that some of the best recipes come from family *ricettari* – recipe collections. These are recipes for dishes that are suited to home cooking, and have been tested and improved over the years by generations of cooks, such as this one.
This cake is gluten-free.

La Torta Sbrisolona
CRUMBLY CAKE

Serves 6

120g almonds
120g granulated sugar
150g plain flour or
 Italian 00 flour
120g coarse polenta flour
grated zest of 1 organic lemon
pinch of sea salt
2 egg yolks
120g unsalted butter,
 at room temperature
unsalted butter for the tin
icing sugar, to decorate

*This cake keeps very well
for several days.*

1 Heat the oven to 200°C/Gas Mark 6.
2 Drop the almonds into a pan of boiling water and boil for 30 seconds after the water has come back to the boil. Drain and remove the skin by squeezing the almonds between your fingers. Spread them on a baking tray and toast them in the oven for 7 minutes or until golden brown. Turn the heat down to 180°C/Gas Mark 4.
3 Put the almonds in a food processor with 2 tbsp of the granulated sugar and process until they are reduced to a coarse powder.
4 In a bowl, mix the flours, the remaining granulated sugar, lemon zest, ground almonds and salt. Add the egg yolks and work with your hands until the mixture is crumbly.
5 Add the butter to the crumbly mixture and work again to incorporate it thoroughly, until the dough sticks together in crumbly mass.
6 Generously butter a 20cm shallow round cake tin and line the bottom with baking parchment. Spread the mixture evenly in the tin, pressing it down with your hands. Bake for 40–45 minutes or until the cake is golden brown and a skewer inserted into the centre comes out dry.
7 Turn out the cake onto a wire rack and peel off the baking parchment. Leave to cool. Before serving, sprinkle the cake with sifted icing sugar.

The word *sbrisolona* is derived from *briciola* (stress on the first syllable), meaning 'crumb', which is what this cake seems to consist of. If you want it less crumbly, you can cut it into slices with a sharp knife when it is still hot. But I find that part of its appeal is its rustic appearance, as well, of course, as its deliciousness. My husband's comment on it, as he munched, was, 'This cake is not just moreish; once you start eating it, you can't stop.'
It is an ideal cake to eat with tea or coffee in the afternoon, or with sweet wine at any time of day.

Panforte
SPICY CAKE FROM SIENA

Serves 8–10

60g candied fruit
60g preserved ginger
150g mixed candied orange,
 lemon and citron peel
60g ground hazelnuts
100g whole hazelnuts
100g almonds
60g walnut pieces
1 tsp ground cinnamon
large pinch of freshly grated
 nutmeg
large pinch of ground cloves
large pinch of freshly ground
 white pepper
large pinch of ground ginger
large pinch of ground
 coriander
4 tbsp plain flour
 or Italian 00 flour
1 tbsp cocoa powder
4 tbsp granulated sugar
4 tbsp clear honey
oil and rice paper for the tin
1 tbsp icing sugar

*Panforte will keep for at
least 2–3 months.*

Panforte is one of the most ancient dolci. A reference to 'a spicy and honeyed bread' brought back to Siena from the Middle East appears in Dante's *Inferno*. It is the traditional Christmas cake of Siena, but is now available all the year round.

There are two kinds of panforte – a white panforte and a black one. The white is the older version. The black was created when cocoa arrived from the New World and became the fashionable ingredient.

My recipe contains a little cocoa and makes a softer panforte than commercial ones. I have also substituted preserved ginger for candied pumpkin, which is not available in the UK. The ginger is an excellent substitute, both for its flavour and for being in keeping with the early origins of panforte, when spices, just arrived from the Orient, were used very prodigally as a show of wealth.

Recipe continued overleaf

SPICY CAKE FROM SIENA

continued

1   Heat the oven to 180°C/Gas Mark 4.

2   Coarsely chop all the candied fruit and peel and place in a bowl. This can be done in a food processor: cut the candied fruits and peel into pieces, put in the food processor bowl and then pulse until all the fruit is in small pieces, but be very careful not to reduce it to a paste.

3   Spread the ground hazelnuts and the whole hazelnuts on 2 baking trays. Toast the ground hazelnuts in the oven for about 5 minutes and the whole hazelnuts for 10 minutes. Shake the trays gently from time to time. Add the ground hazelnuts to the candied fruits in the bowl.

4   Allow the whole hazelnuts to cool slightly and then rub them, a few at a time, in a coarse towel to remove the skin. Place the nuts in a coarse sieve and shake to separate the skin from the nuts. Chop the nuts coarsely and add to the bowl.

5   Chop the almonds (still in their skins) and walnuts coarsely, either by hand or in the food processor (if you use this be very careful not to whiz too much; they must be very grainy, not powdery), and add to the bowl.

6   Put aside a ½ tsp of the cinnamon. Sift the rest of the cinnamon, all the other spices, the flour and cocoa powder directly into the bowl. Mix well.

7   Put the granulated sugar and honey into a small saucepan. Cook over a low heat until the sugar has completely dissolved. Add to the bowl and mix very well with your hands.

8   Line the bottom of a 17.5cm loose-based flan tin with rice paper and grease the sides of the tin with oil. Press the mixture evenly into the tin. Leave to stand at room temperature for 5 hours or longer if possible.

9   Heat the oven to 170°C/Gas Mark 3.

10   Put the remaining cinnamon and the icing sugar in a sieve and sprinkle over the top of the cake. Bake for about 50 minutes.

11   Remove from the oven and leave to cool for 10 minutes, then remove the panforte from the tin and cool completely on a wire rack. When cold, wrap in foil and store.

Pastiera Napoletana
NEAPOLITAN TART

Serves 8–10

250g dried whole wheat,
  to be soaked, or 400g canned
  cooked wheat
600ml full-fat milk
pinch of sea salt
grated zest of ½ organic lemon
  and ½ organic orange
5cm piece of vanilla pod,
  or a few drops of vanilla extract
½ tsp ground cinnamon
300g fresh ricotta
4 eggs, at room temperature,
  separated
2 egg yolks
225g caster sugar
2 tbsp orange flower water
120g candied peel, cut into
  tiny pieces
unsalted butter for the tin
icing sugar, to decorate

For the pastry
300g plain flour
  or Italian 00 flour
6 tbsp icing sugar
pinch of sea salt
grated zest of ½ organic lemon
150g unsalted butter, cut into
  small pieces
3 large egg yolks

1 If you are using dried whole wheat, soak the grains in cold water for 48 hours. Rinse and drain them.

2 Put the soaked wheat in a saucepan with the milk, salt, lemon and orange zest, the vanilla pod and cinnamon and bring to the boil. Simmer over the lowest possible heat for 3–4 hours or until the grain is cooked and tender. Leave it to cool for at least 8 hours (24 hours is better) to allow the grain to swell. Remove and discard the vanilla pod.

3 If you are using canned wheat, just add the lemon and orange zest, vanilla extract and cinnamon.

4 Make the pastry dough: sift the flour, sugar and salt onto a work surface. Mix in the lemon zest, then rub in the butter. Add the egg yolks and knead together briefly to make a smooth and compact dough. (The dough can also be made in a food processor.) Wrap and chill for at least 2 hours.

5 To make the filling, beat the ricotta with the 6 egg yolks. Add the caster sugar, orange flower water, candied peel and grain mixture. Mix very thoroughly.

6 Whisk the 4 egg whites until stiff but not dry. Fold into the grain and ricotta mixture lightly but thoroughly.

7 Heat the oven to 180°C/Gas Mark 4. Butter a 25cm springform cake tin. Roll out about two-thirds of the pastry dough and press into the tin, making sure it is of the same thickness all over the bottom and up the sides. Spoon in the filling.

8 Roll out the remaining dough and cut into long strips. Place the strips over the filling to form a lattice top. Bake for 45–50 minutes or until the filling is set and the pastry is golden brown. Allow to cool and then turn out. Dust with sifted icing sugar before serving.

At Easter time, bakers and *pasticceri* in Naples compete with each other to produce the best *pastiere*, the beloved tart of the Neapolitans, made with whole wheat and ricotta. You can buy whole wheat in tins in good delicatessens and save the long labour of cooking and soaking the grain.

Biscotti e Frittelle
BISCUITS AND FRITTERS

If you open a regional Italian cookery book, you will
find more recipes for biscuits than for any other type
of sweet. This is because, in Italy, sweets tend to be
eaten at any time of day, whereas to have a pudding at
the end of a meal is unusual. Biscuits are often eaten
casually, as a snack, with a glass of wine, sitting round
the kitchen table.

From the vast range of sweet fritters in Italy I have
picked two recipes which I particularly like. Fritters
are amongst the most ancient of foods; in Roman times
they were prepared and eaten in the streets on pagan
feast days, just as they are today at village feasts.
Frying, after all, is the most immediate of cooking
methods, and requires only a saucepan full of oil.

Baci di Dama
LADY'S KISSES

Makes about 35 biscuits

120g ground almonds
120g unsalted butter,
 at room temperature
120g Italian 00 flour
120g caster sugar
1 tsp pure vanilla extract
pinch of sea salt
unsalted butter for the trays
100g bitter chocolate
 (50% cocoa solids)

1 Heat the oven to 180°C/Gas Mark 4.

2 Put the ground almonds in the bowl of a food processor, add the butter and whiz until creamy. Add the flour through the funnel and whiz until the mixture forms a ball. Add 1–2 tbsp of the sugar (this absorbs the oil from the nuts) and process to a fine powder. Add the vanilla and salt and process again until the mixture is very creamy. Transfer to a bowl.

3 With floured hand break off pieces of the dough, the size of cherries, and roll them into balls between the palms of your hands. Place them on buttered baking trays, spacing them about 2cm apart. Bake for about 15 minutes or until golden brown. Leave to cool on the trays for about 5 minutes and then transfer to a wire rack to cool completely.

4 Melt the chocolate in a bain-marie or in a plastic bowl in a microwave oven. When the biscuits are cold, spread a little of the chocolate over one biscuit and make a sandwich by sticking another biscuit to the chocolate.

The name of these biscuits is just as lovely as the biscuits themselves. They are a speciality of Tortona, a town in southern Piedmont.

Le Bisse
S-SHAPED BISCUITS

Makes about 40 biscuits

3 large eggs
180g caster sugar
150ml vegetable or olive oil
grated zest of 1 organic lemon
500g plain flour or
 Italian 00 flour
pinch of sea salt
oil for baking trays

1   In a large bowl, whisk the eggs with the sugar until pale and frothy. Add the oil and lemon zest, then fold in the flour and salt. Knead well. Wrap the dough and chill it for about 1 hour.

2   Heat the oven to 220°C/Gas Mark 7.

3   Grease 2 large baking trays with a little oil.

4   To shape each biscuit, take a little ball of dough and roll it into a sausage shape a little more than 1cm thick and 12.5cm long. Curve into the form of an 'S' and set on a baking tray.

5   Bake for 5 minutes, then reduce the heat to 180°C/Gas Mark 4 and bake for a further 10–15 minutes, or until pale golden. Cool slightly on the baking trays before transferring to a wire rack to cool completely.

A *bissa* is a water snake in Venetian dialect, which explains the name of these little biscuits. They are to be found in any bakery or *pasticceria* in Venice, but they can easily be made at home. Use an unflavoured oil.

I Biscotti della Nonna Caterina
MY GRANDMOTHER'S BISCUITS

Makes about 24 biscuits

2 large egg yolks
2 tbsp rum
120g caster sugar
150g plain flour
 or Italian 00 flour
pinch of sea salt
100g unsalted butter,
 very soft but not melted
butter and flour for the trays

1 Heat the oven to 180°C/Gas Mark 4.
2 Beat the egg yolks with the rum. Add the sugar and beat hard until pale.
3 Sift the flour with the salt and add gradually to the egg and sugar mixture, stirring hard the whole time.
4 Add the butter and beat until the mixture is well blended.
5 Butter 2 baking trays. To form the biscuits, dampen your hands, pick up a little dollop of the biscuit dough and shape it into a round. Place the rounds on the trays, leaving 5cm between each one, as the mixture spreads out a lot while cooking. Bake for 15–20 minutes or until deep gold.
6 Remove the trays from the oven and transfer the biscuits to a wire rack to cool. These biscuits will keep well for a week in an airtight tin.

There is an infinite number of 'Torte della Nonna', but unfortunately none I can claim for *my* grandmother. However, she made these lovely biscuits that are ideal for serving with ice-creams or mousses, or to have with coffee.

Crostoli Trentini
FRITTERS FROM NORTHERN ITALY

Serves 6

150g plain flour,
 preferably Italian 00
1½ tbsp caster sugar
½ tsp baking powder
pinch of sea salt
30g unsalted butter,
 at room temperature
1 large egg yolk
3 tbsp grappa (Italian
 eau-de-vie) or white rum
1–2 tbsp semi-skimmed milk
oil for frying
icing sugar, to decorate

1 Set aside 2 tbsp of flour. Put the rest of the flour on a work surface. Mix in the caster sugar, baking powder and salt. Make a well and put in the butter, egg yolk, grappa and milk. Mix everything together, kneading until the dough is well blended. If it is too hard add a little more milk; if too soft add some of the reserved flour. (You can also make the dough in a food processor.) Knead the dough for at least 5 minutes as you would with bread or pasta dough. It should become smooth and elastic. Make a ball, wrap and leave at room temperature for at least 1 hour.

2 Roll out the dough *very* thinly, using either a rolling pin or, better, a hand-cranked pasta machine. If you are using the machine, roll through the last notch. The thinness of the dough is the secret of good crostoli.

3 Using a pastry wheel, cut the strips of dough into lasagne-size rectangles. Make 3 parallel slashes in the middle of each rectangle.

4 Heat enough frying oil to come two-thirds of the way up the sides of a frying pan or a wok. When the oil is very hot (a piece of stale bread should brown in 50 seconds) fry the dough shapes in batches until pale gold and puffy. Lift the crostoli out of the oil and drain on kitchen paper.

5 Before serving, pile the crostoli on a dish, sprinkling every layer with sifted icing sugar. They are excellent hot or cold.

At Carnival time, every bakery or *pasticceria* in northern and central Italy makes a show of huge trays piled high with puffy golden fritters sprinkled with icing sugar. They are the traditional Carnival fare, made in different shapes in various regions. Thus there are *cenci*, meaning rags, in Tuscany, *chiacchiere*, chatterings, in Lombardy, *galani*, ribbons, in Venice and *sfrappole* in Emilia. The dough varies only a little. What changes is the shape. The original crostoli from Trentino and Friuli are strips of dough tied together in a loose knot, but they are often shaped as I have done here, which is far easier. If you serve them at the end of a meal, hand round a bowl of whipped cream for dipping the crostoli in.

Frittelle di Semolino
SEMOLINA FRITTERS

Makes about 24 fritters

1 litre full-fat milk
100g granulated sugar
pared strip of organic
 lemon zest
120g unsalted butter
pinch of sea salt
250g semolina
3 large egg yolks
oil for frying
2 eggs
225g dried breadcrumbs
icing sugar, to decorate

1 Bring the milk slowly to the simmer with the granulated sugar, lemon zest, butter and salt, stirring frequently to dissolve the sugar.

2 Add the semolina in a slow stream while beating hard with a wooden spoon to prevent lumps forming. Continue stirring and cooking over a low heat for 10 minutes. The mixture will be quite stiff. Draw off the heat and allow to cool for 15 minutes or so. Remove and discard the lemon zest.

3 Mix in the egg yolks, one at a time, beating well to incorporate after each addition.

4 Spread the semolina mixture on a board or flat dish to a thickness of about 2.5cm. Level it down evenly with a damp spatula and leave it to cool completely. You can leave it overnight.

5 Cut the semolina into 2.5cm wide strips and then cut the strips across to make lozenges.

6 Heat oil in a wok or in a deep frying pan to 175°C – hot enough for a cube of stale bread to brown in 50 seconds.

7 Meanwhile, lightly beat the 2 whole eggs in a bowl and spread the breadcrumbs in a dish. Dip a piece of semolina into the egg and then coat with breadcrumbs, patting them into the semolina.

8 Fry, in 2 or 3 batches, to a lovely golden colour and then put into a dish lined with kitchen paper to drain.

9 Serve hot or cold, lavishly sprinkled with sifted icing sugar.

These are also Carnival fritters from northern Italy.
In my home they were always served with apple fritters
and, of course, crostoli (see previous recipe).

Dolci al Cucchiaio
PUDDINGS

In this section I have collected eight recipes for dolci that are served at parties, some famous, some little known, some elaborate and rich, others simple and modest, but all good and typically Italian.

Tiramisù
MASCARPONE PUDDING

Serves 6

150ml strong espresso coffee
3 tbsp brandy
60g bitter chocolate
 (70% cocoa solids)
2 large eggs, at room
 temperature, separated
1 large egg yolk
4 tbsp caster sugar
250g mascarpone
about 20 Savoiardi biscuits

For the decoration
coffee beans
candied violets (optional)

*Savoiardi are available
from Italian delicatessens
and good supermarkets.
If you cannot find them,
make your own sponge finger
biscuits – ordinary sponge
fingers or boudoir biscuits
will not be absorbent enough.*

1   Mix together the hot coffee and brandy. Add ½ tbsp of the caster sugar and mix until the sugar has dissolved. Set aside to cool.
2   Grate about one-quarter of the chocolate and cut the rest into small pieces.
3   Beat the 3 egg yolks with the sugar until very pale and softly peaked. Fold the mascarpone in gradually and mix very thoroughly until the mixture is smooth and does not show any lumps.
4   Whisk the 2 egg whites until stiff but not dry and fold gradually into the mascarpone and egg yolk mixture.
5   Set aside in a small bowl about 2 tbsp of the mascarpone mixture, then cover the bowl and put in the fridge to chill.
6   Take a 1-litre oven dish (oval, round or square, whichever you prefer). Dip a third of the biscuits, one at a time, into the coffee and brandy mixture, turning them over once or twice until they become pale brown and soggy. Lay them, one by one, over the bottom of the dish. Spread about 2–3 tbsp of the mascarpone cream over them and sprinkle with about half the chocolate pieces. Dip more biscuits in the coffee mixture and make another layer. Cover with about half of the remaining mascarpone cream and sprinkle the remaining chocolate pieces over the top. Cover with a final layer of soaked biscuits. Pour any remaining coffee mixture over the biscuits and top with the remaining cream.
7   Cover the pudding tightly and put it in the fridge to chill for about 6 hours.
8   Serve the pudding straight from the fridge, spreading the reserved mascarpone cream over the top of the pudding and sprinkling with the grated chocolate.

A book on dolci would hardly be complete without including the most popular of them all, Tiramisù. Surprisingly, considering its popularity, Tiramisù is a relatively new arrival even on the Italian scene. In the 1970s it was only known in the region where it originated, the Veneto.

Le Dita degli Apostoli
PANCAKES STUFFED WITH RICOTTA

Serves 8–10

For the pancakes
5 large eggs
30g caster sugar
120g plain flour
pinch of sea salt
250ml semi-skimmed milk
butter for frying the pancakes

For the stuffing
600g fresh ricotta
3 tbsp double cream
250g caster sugar
grated zest of 1 organic lemon
grated zest of 1 organic
 orange
grated zest of 1 organic
 clementine
1½ tbsp finely chopped
 candied peel
60g bitter chocolate
 (70% cocoa solids), cut into
 small pieces
2 tbsp dark rum
icing sugar, to decorate

1 To make the pancakes, beat the eggs with the sugar. Mix in the flour and salt and then gradually add the milk while beating constantly. The batter should be fairly liquid. Leave to rest for 1 hour.
2 Meanwhile, prepare the stuffing. Sieve the ricotta into a bowl and fold in the cream and caster sugar. Add all the other ingredients and mix very thoroughly. Chill.
3 Make very thin pancakes in a 28cm pan. (If not using a non-stick pan, grease it lightly with melted butter.) You should get 12 large pancakes.
4 Lay the pancakes on the work surface and spread the stuffing thinly all over each one. Roll them up tightly.
5 Cut each 'finger' into 3 or 4 pieces, place on a dish and sprinkle with sifted icing sugar. They are traditionally served cold.

The odd name of this recipe from Puglia, the heel of the Italian boot, means Apostles' Fingers. I can only suppose the pancakes were given this name because their appearance calls to mind long fingers, raised to give a blessing.
This is the recipe developed by my colleague and dear friend Alice Wooledge Salmon from the original recipe by the cookery teacher Paola Pettini, who showed us how to make this pudding when we went to Puglia for a gastronomic tour.

Crema Mascarpone
MASCARPONE AND RUM CREAM

Serves 4

2 large eggs, separated
2 tbsp caster sugar
2 tbsp dark rum
225g mascarpone
1 tsp lemon juice
12 amaretti biscuits

1 Whisk the egg yolks with the sugar until light and mousse-like, then beat in the rum.

2 Press the mascarpone through a fine sieve and fold into the egg yolk mixture.

3 Whisk the egg whites with the lemon juice until stiff but not dry and fold gently into the mixture until the cream is smooth. Spoon the mixture into long stem glasses and place 1 amaretto on the top. Hand the rest of the amaretti round on a dish. Keep the cream chilled until ready to serve.

Similar to the ubiquitous Tiramisù, this dessert is lighter and more subtle. In my family it used to be called 'La Crema del Principe', and it is indeed a royal dessert, smooth and delicate.

The cream can be prepared ahead of time up to step 3. Add the egg whites no longer than 1 hour before serving. Serve with amaretti biscuits, whose dark, almondy flavour is ideal with this dessert.

La Meringa Farcita
MERINGUE FILLED WITH MARRONS GLACÉS, CHOCOLATE AND CREAM

Serves 6–8

For the meringue
4 large egg whites,
 at room temperature
1 tsp lemon juice
225g caster sugar

For the filling
2 large egg whites
3 tbsp caster sugar
450ml whipping cream
4 tbsp dark rum
225g marrons glacés,
 cut into small pieces
100g bitter chocolate
 (70% cocoa solids),
 cut into small pieces
2 tbsp pistachio nuts,
 blanched, peeled and chopped
 (see page 12)

1 Heat the oven to 150°C/Gas Mark 2.

2 Make an Italian meringue as follows. Whisk the egg whites with the lemon juice until stiff. Put the bowl over a saucepan of simmering water and continue whisking while gradually adding the sugar. Whisk until the mixture is warm, silky looking and forming soft peaks.

3 Draw 2 x 20cm circles on parchment paper as a guide for the meringue shapes. Place the paper on 1 or 2 baking trays. Spoon the meringue over the 2 circles, smoothing it out to the edges of the circles with a palette knife. Place the trays in the oven and bake for about 45 minutes or until the meringue is set. Remove the meringue discs from the paper and allow to cool.

4 For the filling, whisk the egg whites in a bowl until stiff. Place the bowl over a saucepan of simmering water and gradually add the sugar, while whisking constantly. When the mixture is warm, remove from the heat and place the base of the bowl in a basin of cold water to cool. This stiff egg white mixture makes the filling lighter.

5 Whip the cream. Fold in the egg white mixture.

6 Add the rum, marrons glacés, chocolate and pistachios and mix well until everything is evenly distributed.

7 Place one of the meringue discs on a flat dish. Spread two-thirds of the filling over it and put the other disc on top. Cover with the remaining filling. Chill for at least 6 hours before serving.

The meringue in this recipe is Italian meringue, which is less fragile than Swiss meringue made with uncooked egg whites. However, if you find it easier you can make the more common Swiss meringue, as you would for a pavlova.

Mele alle Mandorle e al Vino Bianco

SAUTÉED APPLES WITH ALMONDS AND WHITE WINE

Serves 6

6 equal-sized large apples
 such as Granny Smith
 or other sharp dessert apples
1 organic lemon
60g unsalted butter
3 cloves
150ml Calvados
60g caster sugar, or more
 according to the sweetness
 of the apples
120ml sweet white wine
½ tsp ground cinnamon
90g flaked almonds
300ml double cream
4 tbsp icing sugar, sifted

1   Peel the apples, then cut them in half and remove the cores. Make 4 incisions in the round side of each half, taking care not to cut right through it.

2   Remove the zest from half the lemon using a swivel-action potato peeler, taking care to leave behind the bitter white pith. Squeeze the juice.

3   Heat the butter in a very large sauté pan in which the apple halves will fit comfortably. Add the lemon zest and cloves to the butter and when the butter foam begins to subside, slide in the apples, cut side down. Sauté until golden, then turn the halves over and brown the round side. This will take about 8 minutes. Shake the pan occasionally to prevent the apples sticking.

4   Turn the heat up, pour over one-third of the Calvados and let it bubble away for 30 seconds. Turn the heat down to low and add the caster sugar, wine, lemon juice and 150ml of hot water. Cover the pan with the lid or a piece of foil and cook for 5 minutes. Turn the apples over carefully and continue cooking until they are tender. Cooking time varies according to the quality of the apples; do not overcook them or they may break. If necessary add a couple of spoonfuls of hot water during the cooking.

5   When the apples are ready – test them by piercing them with the blade of a small knife through their thickest part – transfer them gently to a dish using a slotted spoon. Leave to cool.

6   Remove the lemon zest and cloves from the pan. Add the cinnamon and almonds and sauté over a moderate heat for 5 minutes, stirring constantly, until the syrup is thick and the almonds are caramelised. Draw off the heat.

7   Whip the cream. Add the remaining Calvados and the icing sugar and whip again. Spread the cream over a shallow serving dish. Make 12 hollows in the cream with the back of a spoon and lay the apple halves in the hollows, cut side up. Spoon the syrup-coated almonds over the apples. Serve at room temperature.

A lovely dessert, this combines the light, fresh flavour of fruit with the richness of a brandy-laced cream.

Frutta Cotta al Forno
STEWED MIXED FRUIT

Serves 4

2 pears, Comice or Williams
2 apples, Cox's or Granny
 Smith
2 bananas
2 organic oranges
6 pitted prunes
grated zest of 1 small organic
 lemon
3 tbsp light muscovado sugar
150ml robust red wine,
 such as Barbera
pouring cream for serving

1 Heat the oven to 180°C/Gas Mark 4.

2 Peel and core the pears and apples. Peel the bananas and oranges. Slice them all quite thinly, keeping them separate.

3 Lay the sliced fruit in layers in a 1-litre oven dish, arranging it so that each fruit is topped with a different fruit. Scatter the prunes here and there and sprinkle with the lemon zest and sugar. Pour the wine over the fruit and cover the dish. Bake for 30 minutes.

4 Uncover the dish and press the fruit down with a slotted spoon to release more liquid. Bake for a further 15 minutes. Serve warm with the cream.

The simplicity of this pudding should not deter you from trying it. The fruit, well cooked yet still in neat pieces, absorbs the flavour of the wine and its deep colour. Buy prunes that don't need to be soaked.

Zuppa Inglese
CAKE AND CUSTARD PUDDING

Serves 6

150ml double cream
350g best Madeira cake,
 cut into 5mm slices
4 tbsp rum
4 tbsp cherry brandy
2 egg whites, at room
 temperature
5 tbsp icing sugar, sifted
1 tbsp caster sugar

For the custard
500ml full-fat milk
2 strips of organic lemon zest
3 large egg yolks
75g caster sugar
50g plain flour or
 Italian 00 flour

Zuppa Inglese used to be on almost every menu in restaurants within Italy and elsewhere, just as Tiramisù is today. And, like Tiramisù, it can be delicious or disastrous. It all depends on the balance of the ingredients used.

The name Zuppa Inglese – English soup – is a mystery. Like other Italian writers on the subject, I think the pudding must owe its origin to English trifle, which would have been brought to Tuscany and Naples by the English in the eighteenth and nineteenth centuries.

The liqueur Alchermes, used in Italy, is hardly available elsewhere. Cherry brandy is a good substitute.

1   First make the custard. Bring the milk to the boil with the lemon zest and set aside.

2   Beat the egg yolks with the sugar until pale yellow and light. Beat the flour into the mixture and then slowly pour in the hot milk.

3   Transfer the custard to a heavy-bottomed saucepan and place over a very low heat. Cook, stirring the whole time, until the custard is very thick and an occasional bubble breaks through the surface. Simmer very gently for a couple of minutes longer. Place the base of the saucepan in a bowl of iced water to cool the custard quickly. Stir frequently.

4   Whip the cream until soft peaks form. When the custard is cold, fold in the cream.

5   Choose a soufflé dish of 1.75-litre capacity and line it with cling film, which will help in unmoulding the pudding.

6   Line the bottom of the soufflé dish with slices of cake, plugging any holes with pieces of cake. Sprinkle with some rum and spread a couple of spoonfuls of custard over the cake.

7   Cover with another layer of cake, moisten it with cherry brandy and then spread over some custard. Repeat these layers, ending with the cake moistened with one of the liqueurs.

8   Cover the pudding with cling film, place it in the fridge and chill for at least 8 hours, or better still 24 hours, to allow all the flavours to combine.

9   Some 6 hours before you want to serve the pudding, heat the oven to 110°C/Gas Mark ¼. Whisk the egg whites with the icing sugar until stiff. Remove the pudding from the fridge and turn it out on to a round serving dish that can be put in the oven at a low temperature. Peel off the cling film, spread the meringue all over the pudding and sprinkle with the caster sugar. Bake until the meringue is dry and very pale blond in colour, about 20–25 minutes. Allow to cool and then place the pudding back in the fridge to chill for at least 2 hours before serving.

Zuccotto
FLORENTINE CREAM PUDDING

Serves 8–10

75g peeled almonds
75g hazelnuts
3 tbsp brandy
3 tbsp amaretto
3 tbsp maraschino
 or other sweet liqueur
250g Madeira cake,
 cut into 5mm-thick slices
150g bitter chocolate
 (70% cocoa solids)
450ml whipping cream
90g icing sugar, sifted

For the decoration
2 tbsp icing sugar, sifted
1 tbsp cocoa powder, sifted

This is a rich creamy pudding from Florence. Its domed shape is like half a pumpkin (*zucca* in Italian) and it is decorated with alternate brown and white segments, like the cupola of Florence cathedral. This is the classic shape of the Zuccutto, but I am afraid I do not make it like that. As you can see from the photograph, I use an oval fluted mould with a 1.5-litre capacity, which I love, and I do not bother with all the fidgeting of the white and brown segments to resemble the cupola of Florence *duomo*. Instead, I just shower the top with sieved icing sugar and a tablespoon or two of sieved cocoa. If you want, you can use a pudding basin of the same capacity and your Zuccotto will be just as good.

Recipe continued overleaf

FLORENTINE CREAM PUDDING
continued

1   Heat the oven to 200°C/Gas Mark 6. Put the almonds and hazelnuts on separate baking trays and toast in the oven for 5 minutes. Then, with a rough towel, rub off as much of the hazelnut skins as you can. Roughly chop the almonds and hazelnuts and set aside.

2   Mix the 3 liqueurs together. Line the inside of a 1.5-litre dome-shaped mould or pudding basin with cling film and then with cake slices, reserving some for the top. Moisten the cake with most of the liqueur mixture.

3   Melt 60g of the chocolate in a small bowl set over a pan of simmering water (or in a microwave); set aside. Cut the remaining chocolate into small pieces.

4   Whip the cream with the icing sugar until stiff. Fold in the almonds, hazelnuts and chocolate pieces.

5   Divide the cream mixture in half and spoon one portion into the mould, spreading it evenly all over the cake lining the bottom and sides. Fold the melted chocolate into the remaining cream mixture and spoon it into the mould to fill the cavity. Cover the pudding with the reserved cake and moisten it with the rest of the liqueur. Cover the mould with cling film and refrigerate for at least 12 hours.

6   To unmould, place a piece of greaseproof or parchment paper and then a piece of cardboard over the top of the mould or pudding basin. Turn the whole thing over so that the pudding falls onto the cardboard. Remove the mould or basin and peel off the cling film.

7   Now, if you want to make the classic Zuccotto, cut out a 37cm circle of greaseproof or parchment paper. Fold it in two to make a half-moon, then fold this in two to make a triangle. Fold the triangle in two again to make a thinner triangle. Open out and cut out each alternate section, without cutting the paper through at the top.

8   Dust the whole dome with some sifted icing sugar. Mix the 2 tbsp of sifted icing sugar with the cocoa powder. Place the cut-out circle of paper over the dome and sprinkle the cocoa and sugar mixture in the cut-out sections. Remove the paper carefully without spoiling the pattern. Transfer the pudding to a flat round serving dish, using the cardboard for support. Serve chilled.

Gelati, Sorbetti e Gelatine
ICE-CREAMS, SORBETS AND FRUIT JELLIES

I could write a whole book on these sweets, so choosing just a few recipes was quite difficult. Gelati and sorbetti had their origins in Italy, and it was the Italian emigrants who took them to the US, where people have now adopted them and made them their own.

I find that only in Italy can you still find excellent ices in specialist *gelaterie* – ice-cream shops where the ice-creams are made on the premises. The choice is bewildering. Some new favourite flavours, such as tiramisù and zuppa inglese, compete with the lovely old classics, gelato al caffè or al limone. The fruit water-ices are the best because of the strong flavour of the fruit, ripened in the hot sun.

Fruit jellies are now making a welcome comeback on the tables of health-conscious people, and I have included two recipes for them at the end of this section.

Spumone al Cioccolato
FROZEN CHOCOLATE CREAM LOAF

Serves 8

150g bitter chocolate
 (70% cocoa solids)
350ml full-fat milk
4 large egg yolks
120g caster sugar
4 level tsp plain flour or
 Italian 00 flour
4 tbsp strong espresso coffee
300ml whipping cream,
 very cold
12 amaretti biscuits (optional)
120ml Marsala or medium
 sherry (optional)

1 Melt the chocolate in a bain-marie or slowly in a plastic bowl in the microwave, checking every 15 seconds.

2 Heat the milk to simmering point.

3 Meanwhile, beat the egg yolks with the sugar until pale and light. Add the flour and beat well. Slowly pour over the hot milk, while beating constantly. Transfer the custard to a heavy-bottomed saucepan and cook over the lowest heat, stirring constantly, until the custard thickens and some bubbles break on the surface. Cook for a couple of minutes longer, never ceasing to stir.

4 Mix the melted chocolate and the coffee into the custard. Put the base of the saucepan in a basin of cold water to cool the custard quickly. Stir every now and then.

5 Whip the cream. When the custard is cold, fold in the cream.

6 Line a 23cm loaf tin with foil or cling film. Spoon the mixture into the tin and freeze overnight.

7 Remove from the freezer 1 hour before serving. Unmould onto a rectangular dish and cut into slices to serve.

Note: If you wish to cover the ice-cream with amaretti biscuits, crush the biscuits in a bowl then sprinkle them with Marsala or sherry and stir through. Lay them over the spumone just before serving.

A spumone is a kind of soft ice-cream. Spumoni are always moulded in a tin, usually a loaf tin, and served cut into slices like a pâté. This is the recipe for a chocolate spumone of a delicate creamy flavour. You need to use best-quality chocolate with a high cocoa butter content.

This spumone is particularly delicious covered with amaretti that have been lightly soaked in either Marsala or sherry.

Semifreddo di Zabaglione al Caffè
FROZEN COFFEE ZABAGLIONE

Serves 6

3 large eggs, separated
2 large egg yolks
120g caster sugar
150ml Marsala or medium
 sweet sherry
pinch of ground cinnamon
4 tbsp strong espresso coffee
225ml whipping cream
100g icing sugar, sifted
coffee beans and whipped
 cream, to decorate

1　To make zabaglione, I use a stainless steel round-bottomed bowl, which I place over a pan of water. Whatever bowl you use, the bottom of the bowl must not touch the water. Put the egg yolks into the bowl, add the sugar and beat until pale. Add the Marsala or sherry and the cinnamon. Turn the heat on, bring the water to a simmer and continue beating for a minute or so. The mixture will soon become soft and foamy like whipped cream. Remove from the heat and add the coffee. Place in a sink full of cold water to cool. Stir the zabaglione every now and then to prevent a skin forming.

2　Whip the cream and fold into the zabaglione lightly but thoroughly.

3　Whisk the egg whites until firm. Gradually add the icing sugar and continue beating until the meringue forms stiff peaks. Fold it 1 or 2 spoonfuls at a time into the egg yolk mixture.

4　Spoon the zabaglione mixture into a glass bowl or individual glasses and freeze overnight.

5　Decorate with coffee beans and blobs of whipped cream before serving.

A 'semifreddo' cannot freeze hard because of the high sugar content in the meringue. This is why it is called 'half-cold' and why its consistency is so soft and voluptuous.

Sorbetto al Mandarino
CLEMENTINE SORBET

Serves 4

180g caster sugar
pared zest of 1 organic lemon
pared zest of 1 organic orange
300ml freshly squeezed
 clementine juice
4 tbsp freshly squeezed
 orange juice
4 tbsp freshly squeezed
 lemon juice
2 tbsp white rum

1 Put the sugar, lemon and orange zest and 300ml of water in a heavy-bottomed saucepan. Bring slowly to the boil and simmer for 5 minutes. Allow to cool, then strain the syrup.
2 Strain the fruit juices and add to the cold syrup with the rum. Mix well and pour the mixture into an ice-cream machine. Freeze according to the manufacturer's instructions.

A sorbet is not a winter dessert, so it might seem strange to have a recipe for clementine sorbet when clementines are at their very best in December. But a sorbet at Christmas is often a welcome pudding, as it refreshes and cleanses a palate that's slightly jaded from the onslaught of rich food.
This sorbet can also be made with fresh orange juice to which the juice of a lemon is added.

Cassata Gelata
ICED CASSATA

Serves 6–8

600ml full-fat milk
grated zest of 1 organic lemon
5 large egg yolks
150g caster sugar
30g peeled almonds
30g pistachio nuts
150ml whipping cream
30g candied fruit, chopped
1 tbsp icing sugar, sifted

This is the original, home-made, recipe for the cassata that is now sold frozen in supermarkets. It is quite a lengthy dish to make but it is easy, even if you do not have an ice-cream machine. You can substitute bits of best chocolate for the pistachio nuts.

1 In a saucepan heat the milk with the lemon zest until just hot.

2 Put the egg yolks in a heavy-bottomed saucepan, add the sugar and beat with a hand-held electric beater until pale. Gradually pour in the hot milk and place the saucepan over a very low heat. Slowly cook the custard while beating with a wooden spoon until it begins to thicken. At this point, quickly remove the pan from the heat and place it in a sink of cold water. Leave it there to get cold, while giving the custard a good stir every now and then. When it is cold, either pour it into an ice-cream machine and follow the manufacturer's instructions or, if you do not have an ice-cream machine, still-freeze it in the freezer. Leave it until just frozen, but not too hard.

3 Place a 1.2-litre bombe mould (or a metal mould and a piece of foil to act as a lid) in the freezer to chill for 30 minutes.

4 Spoon the custard ice-cream into the chilled mould, lining the bottom and sides evenly but leaving a hole in the middle. Return the mould to the freezer.

5 Put the almonds and the pistachio nuts in a frying pan and dry-fry them until golden. Shake the pan very often. Transfer the nuts to a board and chop them coarsely or do this in a food processor, but be very careful not to blitz them too much and reduce them to powder. You want the nuts to be the size of grains of rice.

6 Whip the cream and fold in the nuts, candied fruit, and icing sugar. Spoon this mixture into the centre of the ice-cream-lined mould and return it to the freezer. Freeze for at least 4 hours.

7 About an hour before serving, remove the lid from the mould, cover the mould with a flat dish and turn them over. Put the mould, on the dish, in the fridge. By the time you wish to serve the cassata you should be able to lift the mould off easily. If the cassata is still frozen onto the mould, dip the mould quickly into very hot water for a few seconds.

Gelatine di Frutta
FRUIT JELLIES

The image of fruit jellies has been debased by the synthetic-tasting jellies made from packets of jelly powder dissolved in water. In Italy these do not exist; the Italians have always made their jellies from the juice of the fresh fruit. These jellies were particularly popular in the Renaissance, when they were made in various shapes and guises to become the centrepieces of lavishly adorned tables.

Here are two fruit jellies, one for the summer and one for the winter. I use leaf gelatine, not gelatine powder, which has an unpleasant gluey flavour, and which dissolves less evenly. Leaf gelatine is sold in the best supermarkets and delicatessens.

Gelatina di Arancia
ORANGE JELLY

Serves 4–6

15g leaf gelatine
150g caster sugar
300ml freshly squeezed
 orange juice, strained
4 tbsp freshly squeezed
 lemon juice, strained
2 tbsp Grand Marnier
4 tbsp white rum

1   Soak the gelatine leaves in cold water for 5–6 minutes until soft.

2   Put the sugar and the strained fruit juices in a saucepan. Bring very slowly to the boil and simmer until the sugar has dissolved, stirring occasionally. Draw off the heat.

3   Put 200ml of water in a saucepan. Lift the gelatine leaves out of the soaking water and squeeze out the liquid. Add to the pan of water and heat gently until the gelatine has dissolved, beating constantly with a small wire balloon whisk. Pour into the fruit syrup and add the two liqueurs. Stir very thoroughly and allow to cool.

4   Grease a 750ml jelly mould with a non-tasting vegetable oil or with almond oil. Pour the mixture into the mould and chill overnight or for at least 6 hours.

5   To turn out, immerse the mould for a few seconds in a basin of warm water. Place a flat dish over the mould and turn the whole thing upside down. Pat the mould and give a few jerks to the dish. The jelly should now turn out easily. Put the mould back on the jelly to cover it and replace the dish in the fridge until ready to serve.

I like to serve this orange jelly with sliced oranges topped with passion fruit. For 4 people you will need 4–5 oranges, 2 tbsp caster sugar and 3 passion fruits. Peel the oranges to the quick and slice very thinly. Put them in a bowl and gently mix in the sugar. Cut the passion fruits in half and with a pointed coffee spoon scoop out the little green seeds and the juice, spreading them all over the orange slices. Make the dish at least 2 hours in advance and keep it refrigerated, covered with cling film.

Buy oranges with full flavour and the right amount of acidity. I use only Italian or Spanish oranges, which have these highly important attributes.

Gelatina di More o di Ribes
BLACKBERRY OR REDCURRANT JELLY

Serves 4–5

15g leaf gelatine
120g caster sugar
5cm piece of vanilla pod
300ml pure blackberry
 or redcurrant juice
4 tbsp Marsala
juice of ½ lemon
150ml whipping cream

1 Soak the gelatine leaves in cold water for 5–6 minutes until soft.

2 Put the sugar, 100ml of water and the vanilla pod in a small saucepan. Bring slowly to the boil, stirring frequently. Simmer for about 10 minutes. Remove from the heat.

3 Squeeze the water out of the gelatine leaves. Add the gelatine to the sugar syrup and allow it to dissolve, while whisking constantly.

4 When the gelatine is thoroughly dissolved draw the pan off the heat. Remove and discard the vanilla pod. Add the fruit juice, Marsala and lemon juice and mix very thoroughly.

5 Spoon the fruit syrup into 4 or 5 bowls. Chill in the fridge for at least 6 hours.

6 Whip the cream and drop a spoonful on top of each bowl. Return to the fridge until you are ready to serve the jelly.

This is a thick jelly, rich in colour and flavour, suitable for serving in individual bowls. I suggest you make your own fruit juice by boiling the fruit for 2–3 minutes and then straining it through a sieve lined with muslin.

LIST OF RECIPES

Antipasti

Pasta

Risotti

Dolci

INDEX

NOTE FOR COOKS

Butter: I use unsalted butter, which is healthier and tastes better than salted. You should use unsalted butter in all sweets

Eggs: I always use free range or organic eggs

Flour: I recommend you use Italian 00 flour, a high-quality flour that is milled very fine, with no additives. It is much easier to work with when making pasta and pastry, and when I use it in dolci recipes I find it gives a more delicate flavour. Italian 00 flour is available in specialist Italian shops and good supermarkets

Lemons and other citrus fruits: I buy organic or unwaxed fruit because I often use the rind

Oil: I use plain olive oil if I am mixing it with butter for frying. Otherwise, I use extra virgin olive oil, especially for dressing salads or when I'm adding it at the end of cooking

Parmesan: I use mostly Parmigiano-Reggiano, particularly when I want to add it grated at the end. But a good padano or even a good mature Cheddar, although less flavourful, are fine for using in stuffings and white sauces

Salt: I use only sea salt, crystal or fine, depending on what I am making and the method used